D1340013

HARRAP'S

English Spelling Rules

Compiled by
G. Terry Page

HARRAP

EDINBURGH
PARIS   NEW YORK

First published in Great Britain 1991
by HARRAP BOOKS Ltd
43–45 Annandale St,
Edinburgh EH7 4AZ

Reprinted 1991, 1993

ISBN 0 245-60144-9

Printed in England by Clays Ltd, St Ives plc

PREFACE

Harrap's English Spelling Rules has three main purposes. The first is to provide a framework for the general improvement of the reader's spelling and, therefore, power of expression in writing. How often do you find that you use certain words confidently and with telling effect in speech yet you shy away from putting them down on paper? *Harrap's English Spelling Rules* is designed to help you bridge that annoying gap, whatever age you are – school pupil, student or adult – and in whatever walk of life.

The second purpose is to cater for all those who will enjoy the opportunity to browse through the labyrinth of rules – and sometimes quirks – on which English spelling is based. This will be of value to the bad speller but, equally, to the good speller who is instinctively right 95 per cent of the time but has lost touch with the rules – and, just as important, the exceptions to them – on which his or her instinctive expertise is founded.

It is thirdly hoped that *Harrap's English Spelling Rules* will provide a reference source and resource basis for those teachers, both in the UK and abroad, who still feel the need to explain or test spelling in the classroom. (The book also, incidentally, highlights the principal differences between British English and American English spelling.)

Harrap's English Spelling Rules begins with a few definitions of terms used later in the book, just in case the reader wants to check them. Then the rules which condition spelling are presented systematically and for ease of reference. Checkpoints at the end of each chapter – and at intermediate points in the larger than usual Chapters 8, 12 and 15 – provide quick self-tests for the reader. Four hundred and fifty Checkpoint questions, with an average of four or five parts, present some 2,000 directly relevant checks or questions.

At some points in this book, pronunciation is used in a very general way to help guide correct choices between similar spellings by giving approximations of the sounds concerned.

CONTENTS

1. Some definitions

The following are a few definitions of grammatical and other terms used in this book. You may find it useful to refer to them from time to time as you use *Harrap's Spelling Rules*. Cross-references between these terms are indicated by *italics*.

adjective
Word that describes a noun. For example, 'fast' in 'fast car' or 'black' in 'black cat'. The *definite article* ('the') and the *indefinite article* ('a' or 'an') are sometimes classified as adjectives.

adverb
Word that tells how, why, when or where, or describes an *adjective*. Thus, in 'the long road back' the adverb is 'back'; in 'the bowling was extremely fast' the adverb is 'extremely'; or in 'it all ended happily' the adverb is 'happily' (adverbs often end in '-ly').

clause
Part of a *sentence* that has its own *subject* and *verb* or *predicate*, but is not the complete sentence. Thus, in 'the server hit the ball hard but the receiver returned it well' the two separate clauses are 'the server hit the ball hard' and 'the receiver returned it well.' Clause is sometimes confused with *phrase*.

conjunction
Word used to connect words, clauses or phrases. Conjunctions include 'and', 'or', 'but', 'for', 'nor', 'yet', 'as', 'as long as', 'as soon as', 'often', 'before', 'since', 'till', 'until', 'when', 'while', 'because', 'why', 'although', 'though', 'if', 'unless', 'in order that', 'so', 'that', 'than'.

consonants

All letters that are not *vowels* (ie all letters other than **a**, **e**, **i**, **o**, **u**). The terms 'hard' and 'soft' consonants are used of **c** and **g** – 'hard' as in 'cut' and 'gut' or 'soft' as in 'Cinderella' or 'Gemma'.

definite article

'The.'

digraph

See *diphthong*.

diphthong

Where two adjacent vowels are pronounced together in a single sound, eg **ea** in 'reach', **ei** in 'conceit', **ee** in 'keep', **ie** in 'field', **oo** in 'hoop', **ou** in 'couch'. These examples are also digraphs, but digraph has the wider meaning of any two adjacent letters, whether consonants or vowels, with a single sound. Thus, other examples of digraphs are **ch** in 'chatter', **sc** in 'scope', **sh** in 'sheep', **th** in 'that'.

homographs

Words spelt alike but having different meanings, eg 'mine', first person possessive, and 'mine', as for coal, gold, etc. See also *homonym*.

homonyms (or homophones)

Words that sound very much alike but have different meanings and, often, spelling. Eg 'affect' and 'effect', or 'access' and 'excess'. Sometimes treated synonymously with *homographs*. Some of the more common ones are listed in Chapter 14.

indefinite article

'A' or 'an.'

noun

Word for a person, place or thing. Thus, in 'Fred played football on the green' the nouns are 'Fred', 'football' and 'green'.

object

Noun, *pronoun* etc, which is on the receiving end of the action of the *verb* in a *sentence*. For example, in 'the player kicked the ball', the object would be 'ball' and can be called the direct object. In 'the back passed the ball to the striker', 'striker' is also an object but an indirect object.

phrase

Group of words usually without a *verb* or *predicate* (unlike a *clause* which does have a verb). Thus, in 'I bring you peace in our time', 'peace in our time' is a phrase.

predicate

The part of a *sentence* that is about or describes the *subject*. It normally includes the *verb* and any *object*.

prefix

Part-word or single letter added to the front of a word or *root*. For example:

        a + typical = atypical
        ante + room = anteroom
        anti + climax = anticlimax
        dis + like = dislike
        il + legible = illegible
        in + eligible = ineligible
        mis + handle = mishandle
        re + turn = return
        un + happy = unhappy

preposition

Word which governs and usually precedes a *noun* or *pronoun*, indicating the noun's relationship to another word. Prepositions include 'on', 'by', 'up', 'over', 'between', 'under', 'before', 'in', 'to', 'about', 'with', 'for', 'at', 'after', 'during', 'through'.

pronoun   Word used instead of a *noun*, usually to avoid
                            repeating it unnecessarily. Thus in the sentence,
                            'Fred also played at Lords, but he made a duck',
                            'Fred' is a noun (a proper *noun*, as it happens)
                            and 'he' the pronoun used instead the second
                            time. Other pronouns include 'I', 'you', 'she', 'it',
                            'we', 'they', 'them', 'who', 'whom', 'which'.
                            Possessive pronouns are 'mine', 'your', 'his',
                            'her', 'ours', 'their', etc − as in 'Fred played at
                            Lords but his bat was broken' ('Fred' the noun
                            and 'his' the possessive pronoun).

proper noun   *Noun* that is the name of a particular person,
                            place or thing: eg 'Fred', 'London', 'Westminster
                            Cathedral', 'Concorde'. In the sentence 'Fred
                            played football at Wembley' the proper names
                            are 'Fred' and 'Wembley' (unlike 'football'
                            which is an ordinary noun). Proper nouns
                            usually begin with a capital, as discussed in
                            Chapter 12.

root   The main part of a word before the
(or stem)   addition of either a *prefix* or a *suffix* to
                            change or modify its meaning. Thus, in
                            'disenchantment' the root is 'enchant' while the
                            prefix is 'dis' and the suffix is '-ment'.

sentence   Self-contained group of words making complete
                            sense in themselves. Usually includes a *subject*,
                            verb and *predicate*, and may include *clauses* and
                            phrases.

stem   As *root*.

subject
Noun or *pronoun* which takes the action or governs the *verb* in a *sentence*. Thus in 'the player kicked the ball' the subject is 'the player'; and in 'the boy thought it was Tuesday' the subject is 'the boy'.

suffix
Word ending added to a word or *root*, changing or modifying its meaning. For example, '-ment' in 'development' or '-ful' in 'joyful'.

syllable
One sound within a word − the only sound in a single-syllable or monosyllable word like 'bird' or 'man'. Multi-syllable words are, for example, 'receive' (two syllables), 'reception' (three), 'receptionist' (four).

verb
Word which indicates action, condition or state of affairs in a *sentence*. For example, in 'Fred played cricket' the verb is 'played', while in 'the bowling is very fast' the verb is 'is'.

vowels
The letters **a**, **e**, **i**, **o**, **u**. They are known as 'short' or 'closed' vowels when pronounced as in 'can', 'hen', 'hiss', 'lot', 'cup'; or 'long' or 'open' vowels when pronounced as in 'cane', 'meter', 'gripe', 'hope', 'dupe'. Two adjacent vowels pronounced together in a single sound form a *diphthong* or *digraph*.

2. ie or ei

First, distinction has to be made between seven different sounds of [ie] or [ei]. These are:

1. the [ee] sound as in 'creek'
2. [ay] as in 'hay'
3. [i] as in 'hit'
4. [eye] as in 'ice'
5. [eh] as in 'best'
6. [uh] as in 'hunt'
7. [oo] as in 'shoe'.

1. [ee] sound

The famous **i** before **e** except after **c** rule applies particularly to this [ee] sound (the same as in 'creek' or 'beak').

It gives us the following **i** before **e** examples when not following **c**:

achieve	diesel	hygiene	reprieve
belief	field	niece	retrieve
besiege	fierce	piece	shield
bier	frieze	pier¹	shriek
brief	grief	pierce	siege
cashier	grievance	priest	wield
chief	grievous	relief	yield

¹*pier* for seaside building but *peer* for aristocratic person.

Exceptions: (**ei** in spite of not following **c**):

either[1]	protein	sheik[1]	weird
neither[1]	seize	Sheila	
plebeian	seizure	weir	

[1]*either* and *neither* are more often associated with an [eye] pronunciation (on this side of the Atlantic, anyway) and *sheik* is often pronounced with an [ay] sound, so they may be rather exceptional exceptions.

The **i** before **e** except after **c** rule gives these **ei** spellings:

ceiling	conceive	deceive	receive
conceit	deceit	perceive	receipt

Exceptions: (**ie** although following **c**): species

2. [ay] sound

For this sound, the same as the [ay] in 'hay' or 'way', the spelling is invariably **ei**, not **ie**. Thus:

beige	feint	neighbour	veil
deign	freight	reign[1]	vein
eight	heir	rein[1]	weigh
feign	inveigh	skein	weight

[1]*reign* as with kings, *rein* as on horses.

3. [i] sound

For this short [i] sound, as in 'hit' or 'bit', the spelling is usually **ei** rather than **ie**. For example:

counterfeit	forfeit	sovereign	surfeit
foreign	forfeiture		

Exceptions:

handkerchief	series	sieve	mischief

4. [eye] sound

For this long [i] sound, as in 'nice' or 'vice', the more common spelling is **ei**, as in, for example:

eiderdown	either	height	sleight
Eiger	Fahrenheit	neither	

Exceptions:

died	hierarchy	hieroglyphics	lied
tied			

Note: Perhaps these [eye] sounds are a bit of a mixture. The alternative pronunciation for *either* and *neither* has been noted under (i) above. *Eiger* and *Fahrenheit* are German words, and *hierarchy* and *hieroglyphics* are of Greek origin.

5. [eh] sound

For this sound, as in 'best' or 'left', the more usual spelling is **ie**. Thus:

friend   lieutenant (see also American [oo] in (7.))

But **ei** is also possible. For example: leisure

6. [uh] sound

For this [uh] sound, as in 'hunt' or 'shunt', the **ie** spelling is invariably used. Thus:

ancient	conscience	patience	patient
proficient			

7. [oo] or [yew] sound

For this sound, the spelling is **ie**:

(in) lieu   lieutenant[1]   review   view

[1]Compare this pronunciation of American origin with the normal British pronunciation in **5** above.

8. Separate sounds instead of a diphthong

In all the above examples the two letters, whether **ie** or **ei**, form a single sound. That is, they form a diphthong or digraph.

But there are other words where the two letters are pronounced separately. In these cases the pronunciation is the key to the spelling, the key to which letter comes first, the **e** (with its [ay] or long [e] sound) or the **i** (usually a short [i] as in 'chin').

Examples:

gaiety (where the **i** is in fact detached from the **e** by forming a diphthong with the preceding **a**) and 'variety'.

Words with **e** before **i** separate sounds include:

deity	reinforce	spontaneity
homogeneity	reiterate	

Note: An [ay] sound followed by an **i** does not necessarily indicate an **ei** spelling. It can also indicate an **ai** spelling: eg. laity.

Examples of words with **i** before **e** separate sounds are:

clothier	crier	medieval[1]	premier
conscientious	fiery	obedience	quiet
copier	glacier	pliers	science

But the **i** and **e** are not of course pronounced separately in 'conscience' earlier in this chapter.

Note: In all but the example of 'conscientious' and 'science' above, the [i] and [e] sounds are separate but the [e] is part of a digraph with **r** to form the [er] sound.

[1]Can also be spelt mediaeval.

✔ Checkpoints

In 1 to 7 below, each group of four words includes two that are spelt incorrectly. Which are they?

1 receive   cieling
   deciet   conceive

2 cashier   piece
   deisel   sheild

3 neice   preist
   wield   conceit

4 lieutenant   liesure
   ancient   consceince

5 veiw   riegn
   eight   weigh

6 sovereign   forfieture
   frieght   skein

7 slieght   niether
   obedient   perceive

In 8 to 14, are the words *in italics* correct or incorrect?

8 The plan was *conceived* in the *beleif* that it would bring *relief*.

9 The *thief* with *conciet* asked for a *receipt*.

10 The *freight* transport was *seized* because it was *overwieght*.

11 The *sovereign invieghed* against what he *percieved* as his *neighbour's deceit*.

12 The *chief* concern was a *belief* that the costs *cieling* would have to be *reviewed*.

13 There was *gaiety* as the old *freinds* enjoyed *their leisure* time.

14 The *greif* around the *bier* produced a *weird* effect.

In 15 to 20, which are the correct spellings?

15 (a) frieze or freize?
    (b) siege or seige?
    (c) sieze or seize?

16 (a) decieve or deceive?
    (b) reciept or receipt?
    (c) deciet or deceit?

17 (a) chief or cheif?
    (b) grievance or greivance?
    (c) achieve or acheive?

18 (a) plebeian or plebeian?
    (b) hygiene or hygeine?
    (c) wield or weild?

19 (a) forfeit or forfiet?
    (b) feint or fient?
    (c) mischief or mischeif?

20 (a) patient or pateint?
    (b) hieght or height?
    (c) liesure or leisure?

In 21 to 25, what are the missing letters, **ie** or **ei**?

21 (a) br_f
    (b) retr_ve
    (c) bes_ge
    (d) gr_vous

22 (a) conc_t
    (b) sh_ld
    (c) rec_ve
    (d) t_r

23 (a) dec_ve
    (b) w_ld
    (c) w_rd
    (d) prot_n

24 (a) fr_nd
    (b) profic_nt
    (c) v_w
    (d) v_n

25 (a) for_gn
    (b) s_zure
    (c) _derdown
    (d) sh_k

See page 216 for Checkpoint Checks

3. Single or double l

1. Dropping the second l in a prefix

If a prefix ending with a double l is added to another word to form a compound word, the double l becomes a single l. For example:

```
all + most  = almost
all + ready = already
all + right = alright
all + though = although
all + ways  = always
full + fill = fulfil
full + some = fulsome
skill + full = skilful
well + come = welcome
```

Note: Skilful is also affected by the rule about dropping the final l in **-ful** (see below). Fulfil is affected similarly, though the Americans do retain the final double l (as they do in 'skillful'). 'All right' is seen at least as frequently as 'alright'. Both forms are acceptable.

2. Full and -ful

The only word ending in **full** that takes a double l is 'full' itself. Otherwise there is always a single l — or **-ful** — when it is the last syllable of a word of two or more syllables. For example, there are the following adjectives:

bashful	fitful	mournful	successful
beautiful	frightful	painful	tearful
careful	fruitful	peaceful	thoughtful
colourful	grateful	pitiful	useful
dreadful	helpful	playful	wishful
dutiful	hopeful	plentiful	wonderful
faithful	joyful	sinful	

fanciful	merciful	spiteful

The same rule also applies to nouns ending in **-ful**, including:

bagful	handful	pocketful	thimbleful
cupful	mouthful	sackful	
fistful	plateful	spoonful	

Similarly, 'till' with the prefix **un-** becomes 'until'.

3. Keeping both ls when adding -ly to words/roots ending in l

There are always two ls if the suffix **-ly** is added to a word ending in l. Thus, if an **-ly** is added to any of these adjectives ending in **-ful** in order to form adverbs, they take **-fully** endings, as follows:

bashfully	helpfully	successfully, etc
faithfully	peacefully	

The same rules apply when adding **-ly** to other words ending in l, as in the following examples:

accidental + ly = accidentally
actual + ly = actually
beneficial + ly = beneficially
cool + ly = coolly
cruel + ly = cruelly
cynical + ly = cynically
especial + ly = especially
eternal + ly = eternally
eventual + ly = eventually
filial + ly = filially
final + ly = finally
financial + ly = financially
formal + ly = formally
fraternal + ly = fraternally
general + ly = generally
gradual + ly = gradually
incident + ly = incidentally
lethal + ly = lethally

loyal + ly = loyally
occasional + ly = occasionally
paternal + ly = paternally
personal + ly = personally
principal + ly = principally
radical + ly = radically
real + ly = really
social + ly = socially
tactical + ly = tactically
total + ly = totally
usual + ly = usually

4. Single l when adding -ly in general
(but with some complications after y, ic, ble and ple)

When adding **-ly** to a word — perhaps to convert an adjective into
an adverb or a noun into an adjective — this is usually simple and
straightforward irrespective of whether the word ends with a
vowel or a consonant. For example:

complete + ly = completely
definite + ly = definitely
desperate + ly = desperately
dexterous + ly = dexterously
extreme + ly = extremely
familiar + ly = familiarly
fortunate + ly = fortunately
friend + ly = friendly
humorous + ly = humorously
immediate + ly = immediately
independent + ly = independently
interesting + ly = interestingly
jubilant + ly = jubilantly
latter + ly = latterly
lone + ly = lonely
love + ly = lovely
quick + ly = quickly
quiet + ly = quietly
rigorous + ly = rigorously

    separate + ly = separately
    similar + ly = similarly
    sincere + ly = sincerely
    staunch + ly = staunchly
    stupid + ly = stupidly
    vigorous + ly = vigorously
    vivid + ly = vividly

But there are at least some complications in the form of the following four groups of exceptions, i) to iv).

Exceptions:

i)   *Adding **-ly** after **y***

When the **-ly** suffix is added to a word or stem ending in **y**, this latter **y** changes to **i**. Thus:

    busy + ly = busily
    crazy + ly = crazily
    fancy + ly = fancily
    flabby + ly = flabbily
    greedy + ly = greedily
    happy + ly = happily
    hazy + ly = hazily
    hungry + ly = hungrily
    merry + ly = merrily
    momentary + ly = momentarily
    necessary + ly = necessarily
    ordinary + ly = ordinarily
    ready + ly = readily
    shabby + ly = shabbily
    steady + ly = steadily

ii) *Adding **-ly** after **ic***

A word ending in **ic** adds **-ally**, instead of plain **-ly**, to become **-ically**. In most cases, though not all, this is evident from the way in which the word is pronounced. Examples of this spelling include:

    analytic + ally = analytically

athletic + ally = athletically
and so on:

automatically	fantastically	scholastically
basically	frantically	scientifically
characteristically	heroically	specifically
comically	historically	statistically
critically	horrifically	stoically
cynically	hygienically	symmetrically
democratically	hysterically	terrifically
drastically	pathetically	tragically
eccentrically	rhythmically	
enthusiastically	scenically	

Note: Public is an exception to the exceptions: it becomes publicly, NOT publically.

iii) **-ble** becomes **-bly**, and **-ple** becomes **-ply**

Adjectives ending in **-ble** change the **-e** to **-y** to achieve an **-ly** adverbial ending. So do those ending in **-ple**. For example:

ample − amply
capable − capably
despicable − despicably
durable − durably
favourable − favourably
forgivable − forgivably
humble − humbly
incredible − incredibly
intelligible − intelligibly
irresistible − irresistibly
irritable − irritably
justifiable − justifiably
knowledgeable − knowledgeably
legible − legibly
noticeable − noticeably
possible − possibly
probable − probably
remarkable − remarkably
responsible − responsibly

      supple − supply
      terrible − terribly
      uncontrollable − uncontrollably
      unforgettable − unforgettably
      valuable − valuably

The same thing happens to subtle − subtly.

iv) One-off exceptions

      true + ly = truly
      due + ly = duly
      whole + ly = wholly
      dull + ly = dully
      full + ly = fully

5. Double l before a suffix beginning with a vowel

Almost invariably, if a word ends with l, and irrespective of where the stress falls in it, the l is doubled before a suffix beginning with a vowel. Such words include:

	-ed	*-er*	*-ing*	*others*
annul	annulled		annulling	
appal	appalled		appalling	
apparel	apparelled		apparelling	
bevel	bevelled		bevelling	
cancel	cancelled		cancelling	cancellation
channel	channelled		channelling	
chisel	chiselled	chiseller	chiselling	
compel	compelled	compeller	compelling	compellable
counsel	counselled		counselling	
cudgel	cudgelled		cudgelling	
enrol	enrolled	enroller	enrolling	
expel	expelled	expeller	expelling	expellable
extol	extolled	extoller	extolling	
fulfil	fulfilled	fulfiller	fulfilling	
grovel	grovelled	groveller	grovelling	
impel	impelled	impeller	impelling	
initial	initialled		initialling	
install	installed	installer	installing	installation

	-ed	*-er*	*-ing*	*others*
instil	instilled	instiller	instilling	instillation
kennel	kennelled		kennelling	
label	labelled		labelling	
level	levelled	leveller	levelling	
libel	libelled	libeller	libelling	libellous
marshal	marshalled		marshalling	
marvel	marvelled	marveller	marvelling	marvellous
model	modelled	modeller	modelling	
panel	panelled		panelling	panellist
parcel	parcelled		parcelling	
propel	propelled	propeller	propelling	propellant (noun)
				propellent (adjective)
quarrel	quarrelled	quarreller	quarrelling	
revel	revelled	reveller	revelling	
rival	rivalled		rivalling	
shovel	shovelled	shoveller	shovelling	
signal	signalled	signaller	signalling	signally
trammel	trammelled		trammelling	
travel	travelled	traveller	travelling	
tunnel	tunnelled	tunneller	tunnelling	

Note: i) Unrivalled, untrammelled, etc, as rivalled, trammelled, etc.

ii) l is unlike other consonants (see Chapter 5, page 41) in that the l doubles before a vowel, as in the above examples, whether the word or root is single-syllable or multi-syllable, and wherever the stress lies if the word is multi-syllable.

iii) Install is unusual among British spellings in having a final -ll.

iv) *American difference.* The doubling or not doing so of the l can be one of the differences between British and American spelling. For example, the American signaled, signaler, signaling, traveled, traveling instead of the above British spellings.

Exceptions:

The **l** does not double before a vowel in the following examples:

appeal − appealed, appealing
devil − devilish
loyal − loyalist
parallel − paralleled, paralleling
signal − signalise (ize)
travel − travelogue

Derivatives of appeal retain a single **l** in line with a general rule that a consonant does not double after two vowels.

6. Single l before a suffix beginning with a consonant

If a word or root ending with **l** adds a suffix beginning with a consonant, it keeps a single **l**.

For instance, with words already used above in **5.** to illustrate what happens with suffixes beginning with a vowel, the following happens when suffixes begin with a consonant:

annul − annulment	instil − instilment
compel − compulsion	quarrel − quarrelsome
enrol − enrolment	revel − revelry
expel − expulsion	rival − rivalry
fulfil − fulfilment	shovel − shovelful
install − instalment	signal − signalman

Note: i) Compel and expel are unusual in making a vowel change, **e** to **u**, to become compulsion and expulsion respectively.

ii) Install-instalment is an example of a word ending with a double **l** reducing it to a single **l** before a suffix beginning with a consonant, as in the examples at the beginning of this chapter (almost, skilful, etc). Other examples include:

chill + blain = chilblain
will + full = wilful
thrall + dom = thraldom

Checkpoints

In 1 to 12 below, are words *in italics* correct or incorrect?

1   *Eternaly gratefull*, the political meeting withdrew its threat of
     expelsion and sent *fraternal* greetings.

2   A *fistful* of dollars would have been *immediately usefull*.

3   *Irritably* and *cynically*, he behaved *allmost despicabley*.

4   *Unfortunatly*, the rain was *allready* falling when they *eventually*
     arrived.

5   Their confidence was *ampley* justified by the *wholy peaceful*
     reception.

6   A *cupful* of the beverage was *readily* and *hungryly wellcomed* by the
     visitors.

7   *Hopefully* and sometimes *franticly*, the team kept trying *untill* the
     finall whistle.

8   The band was *colourfuly* attired but *dreadfully* and *publically* out of
     step.

9   *Unhappilly*, it was *probably* the first time the batsmen had faced
     truely fast bowling.

10   The people were *busily* and *enthusiasticly* engaged in *democratically*
     electing their representatives.

11   It seemed *extremley unlikelly* the event would be *cancelled* in such
     marvelous weather.

12   The prisoners *chiseled* the stonework loose and *jubilantly traveled*
     through the *tunnell*.

In 13 to 20, which are the correct spellings?

13 a) faithful or faithfull?
   b) faithfuly or faithfully?
   c) sackful or sackfull?

14 a) fruitfull or fruitful?
   b) bashfully or bashfuly?
   c) totall or total?

15 a) till or til?
   b) untill or until?
   c) fulfil or fullfill?

16 a) although or allthough?
   b) playful or playfull?
   c) wishfully or wishfuly?

17 a) gratefully or greatfuly?
   b) spoonful or spoonful?
   c) tearfuly or tearfully?

18 a) filial or filiall?
   b) filialy or filially?
   c) fullsome or fulsome?

19 a) fuly or fully?
   b) handful or handfull?
   c) spiteful or spitefull?

20 a) hopefully or hopefuly?
   b) generally or generaly?
   c) skillfuly or skilfully?

21 a) definitley or definitely?
   b) accidentaly or accidentally?
   c) heroically or heroicly?

22 a) busly or busily?
   b) fancyfully or fancifully?
   c) basically or basicly?

23 a) vigorously or vigorouslly?
   b) coolly or cooly?
   c) playfully or playfuly?

24 a) flabbyly or flabbily?
   b) suppley or supply?
   c) bevelled or beveled?

25 a) channelling or channeling?
   b) parallelling or paralleling?
   c) signaler or signaller?

26 a) signalman or signallman?
   b) signaly or signally?
   c) rivalry or rivallry?

27 a) skillfull or skilful?
27 b) wilfully or wilfuly?
   c) shovellfull or shovelful?

28 a) carefuly or carefully?
   b) desperatelly or desperately?
   c) quarrelsome or
      quarrellsome?

29 a) compeller or compeler?
   b) fulfillment or fulfilment?
   c) chilblain or chillblain?

30 a) enrollment or enrolment?
   b) annulment or annullment?
   c) compelsion or compulsion?

See page 218 for Checkpoint Checks

4 Adding a suffix after a silent e and other vowels

What happens to the silent **e** depends very much on whether the suffix you are adding begins with a vowel (eg **-ing** and **-able**) or a consonant (eg **-ful** and **-ment**). There is usually no change with other vowels.

1. Drop the e if the suffix begins with a vowel

If a suffix begins with a vowel, the general rule is to drop the silent **e** at the end of the root. Take the following examples with the suffixes **-able**, **-acy**, **-ed**, **-ible**, **-ing** and **-is**.

a) Dropping the e before **-able**

adore – adorable
advise – advisable
analyse – analysable
argue – arguable
ascribe – ascribable
atone – atonable
believe – believable
bribe – bribable
conceive – conceivable
confine – confinable
console – consolable
create – creatable
cure – curable
date – datable
debate – debatable
decline – declinable
define – definable

describe – describable
desire – desirable
drive – drivable
endorse – endorsable
excite – excitable
excuse – excusable
fine – finable
forgive – forgivable
improve – improvable
inflate – inflatable
love – lovable
machine – machinable
mistake – mistakable
move – movable
palate – palatable
persuade – persuadable
prescribe – prescribable

prove − provable	remove − removable
receive − receivable	store − storable
recline − reclinable	trade − tradable
reconcile − reconcilable	tune − tunable

Note: i) Inadvisable, unbelievable, inconceivable, etc, follow above rule in same way as advisable, believable, conceivable, etc.

ii) Tunable can also be tuneable, like the exceptions below.

Exceptions:

There are exceptional words or roots that keep the silent **e** before **-able**. Most of these exceptions are listed below, and the quick way to deal with them is probably to try to memorise them or have this list by you for reference. There are no differences in pronunciation to help you in most cases.

However, it may be useful to remember that, where **c** or **g** precedes the **e**, the latter is normally retained if pronunciation of the **c** or **g** is soft (as in hence or gesture) rather than hard (as in cut or gun). For example (note the soft **c** or **g**):

change + able = changeable
manage + able = manageable
marriage + able = marriageable
notice + able = noticeable
peace + able = peaceable
pronounce + able = pronounceable
service + able = serviceable
trace + able = traceable

Bridgeable and knowledgeable could also be included in the above list, the **dg** combining in a digraph to give a **g** sound.

Other examples of retaining the **e** include the following. Note that though the **e** is retained with these words when they take the suffix **-able**, it is dropped with the suffix **-ing** (as do the verb forms in the above list − eg to become bridging, changing, managing, noticing, servicing, tracing).

blame + able = blameable   *although*   blame + ing = blaming
give + able = giveable   *although*   give + giving = ing

hire + able = hireable	*although*	hire + ing = hiring
like + able = likeable	*although*	like + ing = liking
name + able = nameable	*although*	name + ing = naming
sale + able = saleable		
size + able = sizeable	*although*	size + sizing = ing
time + able = timeable	*although*	time + ing = timing

Note: i) *American difference* − hirable instead of hireable.

ii) Less commonly, some UK dictionaries allow hirable or salable.

b) Dropping the **e** before **-acy**

conspire + acy = conspiracy
supreme + acy = supremacy

Words or roots ending in **-ate** can lose the **e** in a conversion of **-te** to **-cy**. Thus:

magistrate − magistracy   pirate − piracy

c) Dropping the **e** before **-ed**

age − aged	humanize − humanized[1]
analyse − analysed	necessitate − necessitated
balance − balanced	negotiate − negotiated
devise − devised	paralyse − paralysed
disguise − disguised	prejudice − prejudiced
excite − excited	toe − toed

[1]The **ise** spelling is equally acceptable.

Guarantee, guaranteed and agree, agreed are also examples of dropping an **e** but in fact both before and with the **-ed** the double **ee** forms a digraph or diphthong pronounced as a single sound.

d) Dropping the **e** before **-ible**

collapse − collapsible	response − responsible
reduce − reducible	reverse − reversible
reproduce − reproducible	sense − sensible

e) Dropping the **e** before **-ing**

Blaming, giving, hiring, liking, naming, sizing and timing have already been noted on pages 33-4 as examples of the **e** being dropped before **-ing** (in order to contrast this with what happens with these roots before **-able**). Other examples of dropping the **e** before **-ing** are:

achieve − achieving	fine − fining
adore − adoring	forgive − forgiving
advise − advising	frame − framing
amuse − amusing	grieve − grieving
analyse − analysing	improve − improving
announce − announcing	inflate − inflating
argue − arguing	intrigue − intriguing
ascribe − ascribing	judge − judging
atone − atoning	love − loving
become − becoming	machine − machining
believe − believing	manage − managing
bribe − bribing	mistake − mistaking
bridge − bridging	move − moving
cajole − cajoling	notice − noticing
charge − charging	penetrate − penetrating
come − coming	persuade − persuading
confine − confining	prescribe − prescribing
console − consoling	pronounce − pronouncing
create − creating	prove − proving
cure − curing	rate − rating
date − dating	receive − receiving
debate − debating	reconcile − reconciling
decline − declining	remove − removing
define − defining	restore − restoring
describe − describing	service − servicing
desire − desiring	shake − shaking
discharge − discharging	shine − shining
drive − driving	shove − shoving
drone − droning	solve − solving
educate − educating	store − storing
evade − evading	trace − tracing
excite − exciting	trade − trading
excuse − excusing	tune − tuning

Exceptions:

> But there are a few exceptions where the silent **e** is not dropped before **-ing**. For example:

> singe + ing = singeing (meaning scorching, not singing a song), and whinge + ing = whingeing, thus stressing the soft **g**.

Similarly, tinge + ing = tingeing, with a hard **g**, meaning colouring, and not to be confused with tinging meaning tinkling. Also, dye + ing = dyeing, thereby avoiding confusion with dying (expiring, or departing this life); routeing (drawing up a route) distinguished from routing (defeating); and swingeing (severe) distinguished from swinging (swaying to and fro).

Also: queue + ing = queueing, and:

> hoe + ing = hoeing
> shoe + ing = shoeing
> toe + ing = toeing

Note: The exceptions immediately above apply both to the [oh] pronunciation in hoeing and toeing and to the [oo] pronunciation in shoeing.

> The **e** is also retained when the ending before the suffix is **ye** or **ee**, though this is less a case of the final **e** being silent than of forming a digraph or diphthong with the preceding letter. Thus:

agree − agreeing	foresee − foreseeing
decree − decreeing	guarantee − guaranteeing
eye − eyeing	see − seeing

f) Dropping the silent **e** before **-is**

> analyse + is = analysis   paralyse + is = paralysis

2. Keep the e if the suffix begins with a consonant

> The silent **e** is usually retained before a suffix beginning with a consonant. The following are examples of what normally happens with the suffixes **-ful**, **-ly** and **-ment**.

a) Retaining the **e** before **-ful**

care + full = careful	spite + full = spiteful
hope + full = hopeful	use + full = useful
peace + full = peaceful	waste + full = wasteful

Note: Full becomes the suffix **-ful** as described in Chapter 3, page 22.

b) Retaining the **e** before **-ly**

accurate − accurately	intimate − intimately
approximate − approximately	like − likely
bare − barely	live − lively
complete − completely	lone − lonely
definite − definitely	loose − loosely
desperate − desperately	love − lovely
entire − entirely	rare − rarely
extreme − extremely	spare − sparely
home − homely	sparse − sparsely

Exceptions:

due − duly	true − truly
subtle − subtly	

c) Retaining the **e** before **-ment**

abridge − abridgement	endorse − endorsement
achieve − achievement	excite − excitement
advertise − advertisement	involve − involvement
arrange − arrangement	replace − replacement
commence − commencement	

Exceptions:

Argue + ment = argument, without the **e**. Also,
acknowledg(e)ment may be spelt either way, with or without the **e**,
and abridgement is acceptable instead of abridgement.
Judg(e)ment usually keeps the **e** in common use but lawyers spell it
without the **e**.

3. After other vowels — mainly no change

Final vowels **a**, **i**, **o**, **u** on roots are usually unaffected by suffixes
(what happens with plurals of **o** endings is covered in Chapter 8,
page 74; it sometimes means adding **- es**, not just **-s**). Examples of
roots and suffixes not affected by vowel endings on the roots
include:

	-ed	-er	-ing	others
bikini	bikinied	–	–	
echo	echoed	echoer	echoing	
henna	hennaed	–	–	
mascara	mascaraed	–	–	
mustachio	mustachioed	–	–	
radio	radioed	–	radioing	radioactive
rumba	rumbaed	–	rumbaing	
scuba	scubaed	–	scubaing	
ski	skied	skier	skiing	
taxi	taxied	–	taxiing	
veto	vetoed	–	vetoing	
video	videoed	–	videoing	

Variations in the above rule are adopted French words ending
with an **é** that is acute, and therefore far from silent. They usually
add **-ing** (and also the plural **-s**) but drop the **e** before **-ed** suffixes.
Thus:

appliquéing but appliquéd   chasséing but chasséd
flambéing but flambéd   sautéing but sautéd

Note: But flambéed and sautéed are also usually accepted.

✓ Checkpoints

In 1 to 7 below, each group of four words includes two that are spelt incorrectly. Which are they?

1   adoreing   ascribing
    exciteing   coming

2   hoeing   tingeing
    manageing   traceing

3   adorable   persuadeable
    removeable   reversible

4   marriageable   serviceable
    loveable   reconcileable

5   wasteful   spiteful
    rarley   achievment

6   involvement   advertisement
    excitment   arguement

7   vetoeing   taxiing
    mustachiod   scubaed

In 8 to 15 below, are words *in italics* correct or incorrect?

8   The *rateing* increase was *irreversible* in spite of its bad *timing*.

9   *Foreseeing* trouble from *grieveing* fans, the football club's anxiety was perhaps *forgiveable*.

10   *Singing* loudly, they didn't notice the *burning* and *singeing*.

11   *Shoeing* horses and *hoing* the fields seemed obvious ways of *createing* jobs in the village.

12   The office boy spent more time *eyeing* and *amusing* the office girls than *dischargeing* his duties.

13   It was *noticeable* that he was more *blamable* than *blaming*.

14   The seaplane pilot didn't know whether he was *taxiing* or *scubaing* when he was overtaken by the *bikind* and *mascaraed* water-*skir*.

15 With the meeting *videod* from its *commencment*, the chairman *duely*
   tiptoed more *delicately* than usual through the agenda and with less
   vetoing of points of order.

In 16 to 25, which are the correct spellings and which the incorrect?

16 a) droning or droneing?   21 a) peacable or peaceable?
   b) toeing or toing?   b) peacful or peaceful?
   c) framing or frameing?   c) endorsement or endorsment?

17 a) intrigueing or intriguing? 22 a) traceable or tracable?
   b) judgeing or judging?   b) tracing or traceing?
   c) grieveing or grieving?   c) entirely or entirley?

18 a) shineing or shining?   23 a) judgement or judgment?
   b) tingeing or tinging?   b) acknowledgement or
   c) agreing or agreeing?   acknowledgment?
                                    c) subtly or subtley?

19 a) bridgeing or bridging?   24 a) radiooed or radiod?
   b) abridgement or abridgment?   b) skiing or sking?
   c) queuing or queueing?   c) echoing or echoeing?

20 a) forgivable or forgiveable? 25 a) taxied or taxid?
   b) hirable or hireable?   b) appliquéd or appliquéed?
   c) salable or saleable?   c) echoed or echod?

See page 220 for Checkpoint Checks

5. Adding a suffix after a consonant

The main question is whether the consonant at the end of the word or root remains single or doubles. Different rules apply according to whether the suffix begins with a vowel or a consonant. If it begins with a vowel, there are different rules according to whether the root is single-syllable or multi-syllable and if the latter, according to where the stress lies in the root.

To complicate things further, but not impossibly, there are then some exceptions to the rules.

1. Before a suffix beginning with a vowel

a) Single-syllable words/roots

Double the consonant at the end of a single-syllable word when adding to it a suffix beginning with a vowel. For example:

	-ed	*-er*	*-ing*	*others*
bat	batted	batter	batting	
bed	bedded	bedder	bedding	
beg	begged	–	begging	beggar
clap	clapped	clapper	clapping	
clip	clipped	clipper	clipping	
drop	dropped	dropper	dropping	
fat	fatted	fatter	fatting	fattest
fit	fitted	fitter	fitting	fittest
glad		gladder	–	gladden, gladdest
hit	–	hitter	hitting	
hop	hopped	–	hopping	
prig	–	–	–	priggish
quit	quitted	quitter	quitting	
quiz	quizzed	quizzer	quizzing	

	-ed	*-er*	*-ing*	*others*
rev	revved	–	revving	
rub	rubbed	rubber	rubbing	
run	–	runner	running	
sad	–	sadder	–	sadden, saddened, saddest
ship	shipped	shipper	shipping	
sip	sipped	sipper	sipping	
sit	–	sitter	sitting	
skip	skipped	skipper	skipping	
slap	slapped	–	slapping	
slip	slipped	slipper	slipping	
squat	squatted	squatter	squatting	
stop	stopped	stopper	stopping	
tap	tapped	tapper	tapping	
ton	–	–	–	tonnage
trap	trapped	trapper	trapping	trappings
trek	trekked	trekker	trekking	
sip	sipped	sipper	sipping	

Exceptions (where consonants remain single):

i) *Effect of vowel preceding consonant*

Whether the consonant at the end of a root stays single or doubles often depends on whether a vowel preceding it is pronounced long or short.

Thus: hoped, hoping (meaning wishing) have a single **p** indicating a long [o] as in 'oh'.

But: hopped, hopping (meaning jumping on one foot) have a double **p** indicating a short [o] as in 'loss'.

Similarly: loped, loping (running) but lopped, lopping (cutting off); pined, pining (as in mourning) but pinned, pinning (holding down); shone[1], shining (emitting light) but shinned, shinning (climbing); sloped, sloping (at an angle) but slopped, slopping (spilling); stared, staring (looking) but starred, starring (taking lead).

[1] Example of past tense achieved not by adding suffix but by changing a vowel in the root.

ii) *Where the consonant is* **w**, **x** *or* **y**

Where the consonant at the end of a single-syllable word or root is **w**, **x** or **y**, it does not double before a suffix beginning with a vowel. Thus:

	-ed	-er	-ing
saw	sawed	sawyer	sawing
stew	stewed	–	stewing
tow	towed	tower	towing
tax	taxed	–	taxing
vex	vexed	–	vexing
fry¹	fried¹	fryer	frying
stay	stayed	stayer	staying
toy	toyed	–	toying
try¹	tried¹	tryer	trying

¹Past tense of 'fry' and 'try' change **y** to **i** as well as adding **-ed**.

iii) *Where the consonant is preceded by two vowels*

The consonant at the end of a root does not double either if it is preceded by two vowels. Thus:

	-ed	-er	-ing	others
beat	–	beater	beating	
boat	boated	boater	boating	
creep	(crept)	creeper	creeping	
droop	drooped	drooper	drooping	
group	grouped	grouper	grouping	groupie
haul	hauled	–	hauling	haulage, haulier
heap	heaped	–	heaping	
heat	heated	heater	heating	
hoot	hooted	hooter	hooting	
leap	(leapt)	–	leaping	
loop	looped	–	looping	
sail	sailed	–	sailing	sailor
seal	sealed	sealer	sealing	sealant
seep	seeped	–	seeping	seepage

	-ed	*-er*	*-ing*	*others*
sleep	(slept)	sleeper	sleeping	
soap	soaped	–	soaping	
soar	soared	–	soaring	
treat	treated	–	treating	treatise
trail	trailed	trailer	trailing	

But, in a sense, there are exceptions to this exception – the **u** in **qu** does not count as a separate vowel because it is part of a digraph with **q**. So the consonants do double, as noted earlier, in:

quitting   quizzed   quizzing

iv)   *Where there are two consonants at the end of a root*

If a word or root ends with two different consonants, the last does not double before a vowel. Thus:

	-ed	*-er*	*-ing*	*others*
fast	fasted	faster	fasting	
halt	halted	halter	halting	
search[1]	searched	searcher	searching	searches
turn	turned	turner	turning	

[1]The **h** in **-ch**, **-sh** and **-tch** endings of roots are similarly unaffected by suffixes.

Incidentally, when two different consonants follow a vowel they can conceal whether the vowel is long or short. Thus, it is short in:

banger   lodger   ledger   clock

but long in: danger

v)   *Multi-syllable words/roots before a suffix beginning with a vowel*

A key question is where the stress is pronounced in the word/root – whether on the last syllable or earlier.

vi) Where the stress is on the last syllable of a multi-syllable root

With a word/root of two or more syllables ending in a consonant, the consonant is doubled before a suffix beginning with a vowel if the stress on the root is on the last syllable. This does make sense; you do hang on to the last consonant longer in pronunciation if the stress is on the last syllable. For example:

	-ed	*-er*	*-ing*	*others*
acquit	acquitted	–	acquitting	acquittal
admit	admitted	–	admitting	admittance, admittedly
allot	allotted	–	allotting	allottee
begin	(began)	beginner	beginning	
commit	committed	–	committing	committable, committal, committee
confer	conferred	conferrer	conferring	conferrable
equip	equipped	equipper	equipping	
forget	(forgot)	–	forgetting	forgettable
forgot	–	–	–	forgotten
occur	occurred	–	occurring	occurrence
omit	omitted	–	omitting	
permit	permitted	permitter	permitting	
prefer	preferred	–	preferring	
quarrel	quarrelled	quarreller	quarrelling	
refer	referred	–	referring	
regret	regretted	–	regretting	regrettable
remit	remitted	remitter	remitting	remittal, remittance, remittee, remittent
transfer	transferred	transferrer	transferring	
transmit	transmitted	transmitter	transmitting	transmittable, transmittal

Note: i) The 'others' column might also have included admission, omission, permission, remission, transmission as derivatives of admit, omit, permit, remit, transmit, though the **t** has been replaced by **s**.

     ii) If the same root varies its stress from the last syllable with some suffixes, this affects whether the final consonant is doubled. Thus we have:

> confer, conferred, conferring, conferrable but conference, conferee;
> equip, equipped, equipping but equipage;
> prefer, preferred, preferring but preferable, preference, preferential;
> refer, referred, referring but referable, referee, reference;
> transfer, transferred, transferrer, transferring but transferable, transferee, transference.

     iii) The special case of words/roots ending in **l** — they virtually all double it before a suffix beginning with a vowel, wherever the stress falls — is dealt with in Chapter 3.

     iv) Different rules apply for suffixes beginning with a consonant, as described later in this chapter.

vii) *Where the stress is earlier than the last syllable in a multi-syllable word/root*

    If the stress falls earlier than the last syllable of a multi-syllable word/root ending in a consonant, this consonant normally remains single if a suffix beginning with a vowel is added. For example:

	-ed	*-er*	*-ing*	*others*
ballot	balloted	–	balloting	
banquet	banqueted	banqueter	banqueting	
bayonet	bayoneted	bayoneter	bayoneting	
benefit	benefited	–	benefiting	
bias	biased	–	biasing	
bigot	bigoted	–		
billet	billeted	billeter	billeting	billetee
blanket	blanketed	–	blanketing	

	-ed	-er	-ing	others
blossom	blossomed	–	blossoming	
bonnet	bonneted	–	–	
bracket	bracketed	–	bracketing	
budget	budgeted	–	budgeting	budgetary
buffet	buffeted	–	buffeting	
carpet	carpeted	–	carpeting	
chirrup	chirruped	chirruper	chirruping	
combat	combated	–	combating	combatant, combative
cricket	–	cricketer	cricketing	
discomfort	discomfited	–	discomfiting	discomfiture
docket	docketed	–	docketing	
facet	faceted	–	–	
ferret	ferreted	–	ferreting	
fidget	fidgeted	–	fidgeting	
fillet	filleted	filleter	filleting	
fillip	filliped	–	filliping	
focus	focused	–	focusing	
gallop	galloped	galloper	galloping	
gibbet	gibbeted	–	gibbeting	
gossip	gossiped	gossiper	gossiping	
happen	happened	–	happening	
harvest	harvested	harvester	harvesting	
helmet	helmeted	–	–	
hiccup	hiccuped	hiccuper	hiccuping	
jacket	jacketed	–	jacketing	
journey	journeyed	–	journeying	
junket	junketed	–	junketing	
letter	lettered	–	lettering	
market	marketed	–	marketing	marketeer
offer	offered	–	offering	
packet	packeted	–	packeting	
picket	picketed	–	picketing	
pilot	piloted	–	piloting	pilotage
pivot	pivoted	–	pivoting	pivotal
pocket	pocketed	–	pocketing	pocketable
proffer	proffered	–	proffering	
profit	profited	–	profiting	profitable, profiteer

	-ed	*-er*	*-ing*	*others*
rivet	riveted	riveter	riveting	
scallop	scalloped	–	scalloping	
target	targeted	–	targeting	
trumpet	trumpeted	trumpeter	trumpeting	
wicked	–	–	–	wickeder, wickedish
woman	–	–	–	womanish

Note: i) Generally accepted, and American-influenced, alternatives to biased/biasing and focused/focusing are biassed/biassing and focussed/focussing.

ii) As with single-syllable words/roots earlier in this chapter, those ending in **w**, **x** or **y** do not double this consonant, wherever the stress may fall. This gives, for example:

array, arrayed, arraying
destroy, destroyer, destroyed, etc
guffaw, guffawed, guffawing
relax, relaxed, relaxing

iii) As noted earlier in this chapter, the exceptional case of roots ending in l is covered in Chapter 3. They usually double the l.

Exceptions:

handicap	handicapped	handicapper	handicapping
input	inputted	–	inputting
kidnap	kidnapped	kidnapper	kidnapping
output	outputted	–	outputting
worship	worshipped	worshipper	worshipping

American differences – single **p** in kidnaped, kidnaper, kidnaping, worshiped, worshiper, worshiping.

2. Before a suffix beginning with a consonant

The general rule is to leave consonants as they are when adding an ending or suffix beginning with a consonant to a word or root ending in a consonant. For example:

drunken + ness = drunkenness
keen + ness = keenness
level + ness = levelness
mean + ness = meanness
stubborn + ness = stubbornness
allot + ment = allotment
annul + ment = annulment
commit + ment = commitment
confer + ment = conferment
develop + ment = development
embarrass + ment = embarrassment
equip + ment = equipment
govern + ment = government
harass + ment = harassment
steward + ship = stewardship
pocket + full = pocketful
regret + full = regretful
first + hand = firsthand
by + line = byline
foot + note = footnote
hand + book = handbook
letter + head = letterhead
over + rule = overrule
paper + back = paperback
post + card = postcard
quarrel + some = quarrelsome
revel + ry = revelry
grand + daughter = granddaughter
step + father = stepfather
birth + right = birthright

Note: i) Several of the above words/roots make changes in the final consonant if linked with a suffix beginning with a vowel instead of a consonant, as noted earlier in this chapter.

ii) Words ending in **-ful** are dealt with in more detail in Chapter 3.

Exceptions:

grand + dad = grandad (but the orthodox granddad is also acceptable)

3. When vowels are dropped or changed within words/roots on adding a suffix

There are a few cases where a word/root drops a vowel within it when adding a particular suffix. For example, words ending in **-our** drop the **u** when adding **-ous** (usually to convert a noun into an adjective). Thus:

glamour + ous = glamorous   rigour + ous = rigorous
humour + ous = humorous   vigour + ous = vigorous

American differences − there is no **u** in the nouns in the first place − glamor, humor, rigor, vigor.

Note: Back to British spelling − the **u** in the above words is also dropped before some other suffixes; eg glamorise (or -ize), humorist, rigorism, rigorist.

A dropping of a vowel within the word/root also happens in the following cases, as can be deduced from the way they are pronounced:

announce + iate = annunciate
curious + ity = curiosity
disaster + ous = disastrous
enter + ance = entrance
exclaim + ation = exclamation
generous + ity = generosity
hunger + y = hungry
labour + ious = laborious
proclaim + ation = proclamation
pronounce + iation = pronunciation

American differences − no **u** in labo(u)r

There are also examples like the following where a vowel is changed within a root when a suffix is added.

compel + sion = compulsion
example + ify = exemplify
expel + sion = expulsion

✔ **Checkpoints**

In 1 to 6 below, in each group of four words which two are spelt correctly?

1. fitter   droped
   shipper   ziped

2. stewing   arayyed
   hitting   squater

3. groupped   creeping
   quiting   trailer

4. commited   occurred
   transferred   budgetted

5. picketing   proffered
   targeted   kidnaping

6. meaness   granddaughter
   exclaimation   glamorous

In 7 to 12, which of the words *in italics* are correctly spelt and which incorrectly?

7. He *hoped* that *loping* along quickly instead of *hoping* on one foot would get him there *fasttest*.

8. The flashy sports car driver *reved* the engine, *hooting* his horn and *trying* to get away first.

9. With time *sliping* away and the *batting falling* apart, the team's *staying* ability was being taxed.

10. The light aircraft *soarred* into the air, *shining* in the sun and *transmiting* to the control tower.

11. *Biassed* opinions and inefficient *budgetting handicapped* the organisation's performance.

12. Their *keenness* dulled by *drunkeness*, the *revellers journied joyously*.

In 13 to 25, which are the correct spellings?

13 a) quizzed or quized?
   b) fatest or fattest?
   c) taxing or taxiing?

14 a) arrayed or arayyed?
   b) shoper or shopper?
   c) tried or tryed?

15 a) drooping or droopping?
   b) triing or trying?
   c) acquitted or acquited?

16 a) preferred or prefered?
   b) preferrable or preferable?
   c) quarrelling or quarreling?

17 a) balloting or ballotting?
   b) bigotry or bigottry?
   c) galloper or gallopper?

18 a) budgeting or budgetting?
   b) marketing or marketting?
   c) targeted or targetted?

19 a) regreted or regretted?
   b) transmited or transmitted?
   c) beginer or beginner?

20 a) transfered or transferred?
   b) regretful or regretfull?
   c) harvester or harvestter?

21 a) focused or focussed?
   b) picketing or picketting?
   c) worshiper or worshipper?

22 a) commited or committed?
   b) commitment or committment?
   c) conferment or conferrment?

23 a) glamourous or glamorous?
   b) granddad or grandad?
   c) vigorous or vigourous?

24 a) announciate or annunciate?
   b) laborious or labourious?
   c) enterance or entrance?

25 a) overrule or overule?
   b) stubborness or stubbornness?
   c) kidnaper or kidnapper?

See page 222 for Checkpoint Checks

6. i or y

1. i and y spellings that get confused

Some i and y spellings often get confused, whether pronounced with a long i, as in hire, or a short i as in hiss.

Words with an i spelling pronounced long include:

biannual	bionic	stifle
biennial	bite	stile (*in fence*)
bicep	diet	title
biography	micro	trident
biology	siren	

Words with an i spelling pronounced short include:

binge	citrus	timorous
biscuit	civic	titter
bishop	city	titular
cinema	linchpin	tribune
cistern	mini	tribute
citadel	stick	trickle
citizen	stigma	

Words with a y spelling pronounced like a long [i] include:

cyanide	hype	typography
cycle	style (*manner*)	typhoon
Cyclops	stylus	tyrant
cypress	stymie	tyre (US, tire)
dynamo	typist	xylophone

Words with a y spelling pronounced like a short [i] include:

crypt	cyst	myth
crystal	dynasty	styptic
cylinder	Egypt	Styx
cymbal	gymnast	syrup
cynic	lynch	typical

Words in which either **i** or **y** may be used include:

cider or cyder	sillabub or syllabub
cipher or cypher	silvan or sylvan
dike or dyke	tike or tyke
gipsy or gypsy	tiro or tyro
pigmy or pygmy	

The [ee] sound at the end of a word is usually achieved by a **y** (happy, jolly) or **ey** (valley, volley) ending but in some words (usually of Italian origin) it is achieved by an **i** ending. For example:

cannelloni	graffiti	macaroni
mafiosi	spaghetti	

2. When does adding a suffix change y to i?

When adding a suffix to a word ending in **y**, the **y** remains if it is preceded by a vowel (including when the suffix is **s** to form a plural, as in Chapter 8). But if the **y** is preceded by a consonant, it becomes an **i**. A major exception noted below is that the **y** usually remains anyway if the suffix is **-ing**.

Examples of the **y** remaining because it is preceded by a vowel include:

buy	– buyer, buying, buys
employ	– employable, employed, employee, employer, employing, employment
enjoy	– enjoyable, enjoyed, enjoying, enjoyment
journey	– journeyed, journeying, journeyman, journeys
joy	– joyful, joyous, enjoyable, joys
monkey	– monkeying, monkeys
pay	– payee, payer, payment
play	– playable, played, player, playful, playing
slay	– slayer, slaying
trolley	– trolleyed, trolleying, trolleys

Exceptions:

In the case of the following exceptions, the **y** becomes an **i** in spite of the preceding vowel. Note, however, that the **i** forms a digraph or diphthong with a preceding vowel (so the pronunciation test will help you).

day, daily	lay, laid	say, said
gay, gaiety	pay, paid	slay, slain

Examples of the **y** becoming **i** because of a preceding consonant include the following (for **-ing** suffixes, see exceptions below):

beauty	— beautiful, beautify
busy	— busier, busiest, busily, business
carry	— carriage, carried, carrier, carries
comply	— compliance, compliant, complied, complies
dry	— dried, drier, driest
easy	— easier, easiest, easily, easing
envy	— enviable, envied, envies, envious
happy	— happier, happiest, happily, happiness
harry	— harried, harrier
hungry	— hungrier, hungriest, hungrily
imply	— implication, implied
justify	— justifiable, justification
likely	— likelier, likeliest, likelihood
lonely	— lonelier, loneliest, loneliness
marry	— marriage, married
merry	— merrier, merriest, merrily, merriment
necessary	— necessarily
ordinary	— ordinarily, ordinariness
pretty	— prettier, prettiest, prettily, prettiness
pity	— pitied, pities, pitiful, pitiless
ply	— pliable, pliant, plied, pliers, plies
rely	— reliable, reliant, relied, relies

Exceptions:

Main exceptions are where the **y** is retained before the **-ing** suffix to avoid having two **i**s together (which would be confusing, to say the least). For example: carry + ing = carrying, not carriing!

Other correct examples of **y** being followed by **-ing** are:

comply + ing = complying
harry + ing = harrying
hurry + ing = hurrying
justify + ing = justifying
marry + ing = marrying
occupy + ing = occupying
pity + ing = pitying
ply + ing = plying
try + ing = trying

Other exceptions include: dryer (drying equipment), dryish, dryness, slyness

There are also one or two cases where either a **y** or **i** is correct.

dry + ly = either dryly or drily
sly + ly = slyly or (but unusual) slily

3. Changing ie to y

The usual **y or i** problem − covered above − is knowing when a **y** changes to **i**. Occasionally, however, change is in the reverse direction, from **ie** to **y**, usually to avoid having **-ing** follow **ie**. Thus:

die + ing = dying
tie + ing = tying
lie + ing = lying

✓ Checkpoints

In 1 to 5 below, in each group of three words one is correct and can only be spelt that way, one is correct but also has an alternative spelling, and the third is incorrect. Which is which?

1	gypsy	cyanide	cristal
2	bycep	dike	lynch
3	city	cityzen	tike
4	styfle	pigmy	timorous
5	xylophone	cypher	lynchpin

In 6 to 10, in each group of four words which two are spelt correctly and which incorrectly?

6	journied	joyous
	paiment	enjoyment
7	busyly	relyant
	prettily	paid
8	playable	monkies
	complied	dryer
9	dayly	slaying
	slayn	dryness
10	laid	spaghetty
	hungryly	gaiety

In 11 to 15, which of the words *in italics* are correctly spelt and which incorrectly?

11 The *dryest* weather on record made the *cyder* harvest *unreliable* and hardly a scene of *silvan* splendour.

12 *Complyance* with the law *necessarily implyed* reduced *meryment* when driving a *mini*.

13 *Tying* the loose ends together, the chairman *drily* commented that he hoped to see everyone *complying* with his ruling.

14 He tried to use *plyers* to repair the *linchpins* of the six-*cylinder* car.

15 The *unemployed tipist* was *harryed* into helping the *cypher*-breakers.

In 16 to 18, which are the correct spellings?

16 a) trolleys or trollies?
  b) citadel or citydel?
  c) bicep or bycep?

17 a) tire or tyre?
  b) cymbal or cimbal?
  c) payd or paid?

18 a) pityless or pitiless?
  b) slyly or slily?
  c) dying or dyeing?

In 19 to 25, what are the missing letters, **i** or **y**?

19 a) c_anide   b) cr_pt
  c) c_stern   (d) p_gmy

20 a) s_rup   b) Eg_pt
  c) d_ke   (d) C_clops

21 a) s_phon   b) t_rant
  c) c_trus   (d) tr_dent

22 a) t_tter   b) t_phoon
  c) enyo_able   (d) monke_s

23 a) jo_ous   b) sla_n
  c) lonel_ness   (d) merr_r

24 a) da_ly   b) ga_ety
  c) pla_er   (d) sla_ing

25 a) marr_age   b) happ_ly
  c) pl_able   (d) carr_er

See page 224 for Checkpoint Checks

7. c, k or ck, or sometimes s

1. Word beginnings — hard or soft, c or k

Confusion can arise over whether to use **c** or **k** for a hard initial [c] sound, as in cattery or kennel. If the letter precedes either the vowels **a**, **o**, **u** or the consonants **l** or **r**, it will normally be a **c**. Thus:

cab	cat	close	counter
cabin	cathode	cloud	crew
cable	cause	clump	cricket
cad	clarity	clutch	crisp
cafe	clench	cod	criterion
calendar	clergy	collapse	crook
call	clerk	computer	croupier
can	climate	conduct	crunch
capital	clinch	connoisseur	cub
care	clipper	cost	cuddle
carve	clock	cot	custody
cast	cloister	court	cut

But for a hard [c] sound before **e** or **i**, a **k** is usual. Thus:

kebab	kennel	kill	kiosk
keel	kerb[1]	kilometre	kiss
keen	kettle	kilt	kitten
keep	key	kind	
keg	kidney	king	

[1]Kerb may also be spelt curb, thus orthodoxly taking **c** in conjunction with **u**.

Exceptions (all foreign-derived from many different
languages) where **k** is used before **a**, **o**, **u**, **l** or **r** include:

kaftan[1]	kaolin	kleptomaniac	Kremlin
kaiser	kapok	koala	krona
kaleidoscope	karate	kosher	kudos
kamikaze	kayak	kowtow	
kangaroo	klaxon	kraal	

[1]Kaftan can also be spelt caftan.

Where a soft [c] sound (as opposed to the above hard [c] sounds) comes before an **e** or **i**, a **c** is usually the correct letter. For example:

cease	Celsius	century	city
cedar	cement	cinder	cygnet
ceiling	cemetery	circle	cymbals
celebrity	census	circulate	cynic
celery	central	circus	Cypriot
cellar	centre	cistern	cyst

For the soft [c] sound, there can sometimes be confusion between **c** and **s**. Even though followed by an **e** or **i**, the following words, for example, use **s** :

secede	senior	session	signature
second	sense	several	silicon
secretary	sentry	sibilant	sister
semantic	septet	side	
senate	sequel	sign	

When followed by any of the other vowels — **a, o, u** — the normal provider of the soft [c] sound is an **s**. Thus:

Sabbath	saint	sash	subconscious
sabotage	salary	savage	subdue
sachet	sale	sodden	subsonic
sack	sallow	soggy	such
sad	same	solid	sudden
safari	sanction	solitary	summer
safe	sandwich	sound	
sail	sarong	sow	

2. When to add k to c before adding a suffix

It depends largely on the suffix. A word ending in **c** will usually add a **k** before a suffix that begins with an **e**, **i** or **y**. This maintains the hard sound of the **c**. Thus:

	-ed	-ing	other, **e**, **i**, **y**
bivouac	bivouacked	bivouacking	
frolic	frolicked	frolicking	frolicky
mimic	mimicked	mimicking	
panic	panicked	panicking	panicky
picnic	picnicked	picnicking	picnicker
politic	politicked	politicking	politicker
traffic	trafficked	trafficking	trafficker

Exceptions:

arc, arced, arcing
zinc, zinced, zincing, zincify

When the suffix begins with other than **e**, **i** or **y**, an intervening **k** is unnecessary. The **c** remains hard without it. Thus the words or roots used above with **e**, **i** and **y** give the following words with other suffixes:

frolicsome mimicry trafficator trafficless politics

This rule applies similarly to the following roots and suffixes:

automatic, automatically
dramatic, dramatically, dramatics
frantic, frantically
heroic, heroically, heroics
mechanic, mechanical, mechanically
music, musical, musically
periodic, periodical, periodically
poetic, poetical, poetically

3. ck after short vowels, but with exceptions

The principal use of **ck** (other than before **-ed**, **- ing**, etc, in **2.** above) is after a short vowel; that is, **a** as pronounced in back; **e** as in neck; **i** as in sick; **o** as in sock; and **u** as in truck. For example:

attack	knickers	racket	snack
block	lock	rickety	speckled
bracket	locket	rock	sprocket
bucket	muck	rocket	sucker
cockle	neck	sack	trick
crock	package	sacking	truck
duck	packet	shack	whack
flick	picket	shock	wicket
gimmick	plucky	shocking	wreck
jackal	pucker	sick	

Exceptions:

i) *Multi-syllable words ending in* **-ac** *or* **-ic**, *such as:*

Adriatic	frantic	music	terrific
almanac¹	frenetic	optic	topic
anarchic	historic	Pacific	traffic
Atlantic	horrific	panic	traumatic
automatic	lunatic	poetic	tropic
bivouac	mechanic	politic	zodiac
dramatic	meteoric	soporific	
erotic	mimic	tactic	

¹ Also sometimes spelt almanack

ii) *A small number of words using* **k** *only (from a variety of overseas origins, from Malaysian to Eskimo, from Turkish to Afrikaans). They include:*

kapok	kayak	kiosk	Kodak
trek	yashmak		

iii) *The* **c** *after a short vowel can also be found in multi-syllable words that do not have an associated word ending in* **c**. *Thus:*

icicle	nautical	robotics

Icicle, incidentally, has two **c**s following vowels, but the first is soft (as in ice).

✔ Checkpoints

In 1 to 7 below, in each group of four words which two are spelt correctly and which incorrectly? Correct the latter.

1 klench   calendar
   capok   croupier

2 cowtow   sensus
   celery   kaleidoscope

3 picnicker   kod
   ciosk   computer

4 panick   panicked
   trafficing   trafficker

5 sygnet   almanac
   jacal   mechanic

6 yashmack   icicle
   lunatic   zodiack

7 ceptet   cibilant
   cricket   signature

In 8 to 13, which of the words *in italics* are correctly spelt and which incorrectly? Correct the latter.

8 *Frolicking* around *periodickally* made no sense while *bivouacing* on the *sogy* mountainside.

9 The *connoisseur* rated the *cebabs* a *cut* above the usual *snak*.

10 On such a *tricky wiket* a *quik century* would have been a bit of a *shock*, but a tribute to the batsman's ability to *whac* the ball.

11 The *erotick* dancing displayed on the *kathode* ray tube had a *traumatic* effect on their *conduct*.

12 *Dramatickally panicy karate* chops did not seem appropriate in a *kamickaze* pilot.

13 The *kilometres* of *trafficless* streets echoed to the *raket* of *symbals* as the *celebrations* got under way and the great *trek* through the *sity* reached *terrific* proportions.

In 14 to 20, which are the correct spellings?

14 (a) mimic or mimick?
   (b) mimicing or mimicking?
   (c) mimickry or mimicry?

15 (a) heroic or heroick?
   (b) capital or kapital?
   (c) caftan or kaftan?

16 (a) cudos or kudos?
   (b) cynic or cynick?
   (c) cyst or syst?

17 (a) braket or bracket?
   (b) Atlantic or Atlantick?
   (c) gimmick or gimmic?

18 (a) politicing or politicking?
   (b) speckled or spekled?
   (c) politics or politicks?

19 (a) kurb or curb?
   (b) robotics or roboticks?
   (c) sarong or carong?

20 (a) zinced or zincked?
   (b) cecede or secede?
   (c) trek or treck?

See page 226 for Checkpoint Checks

8. Forming plurals

1. Plurals that simply add an s

Often, adding an **s** is all you need do to form a plural. This is a particularly safe rule for words ending in **e**, such as the following:

absence, absences	home, homes
aerodrome, aerodromes	horse, horses
angle, angles	isle, isles
annexe, annexes	licence, licences
antidote, antidotes	magazine, magazines
bicycle, bicycles	niece, nieces
centre, centres	parachute, parachutes
chocolate, chocolates	satellite, satellites
divergence, divergences	scene, scenes
entrance, entrances	theatre, theatres
file, files	trestle, trestles
giraffe, giraffes	venture, ventures

American differences – Center(s) for centre(s); theater(s) for theatre(s).

Many other straightforward nouns also simply add an **s**. For example:

airfield, airfields	girl, girls
airport, airports	ghost, ghosts
arrival, arrivals	manager, managers
balloon, balloons	nephew, nephews
book, books	printer, printers
boy, boys	receipt, receipts
circuit, circuits	ribbon, ribbons
colour, colours	shield, shields
computer, computers	typewriter, typewriters
contract, contracts	wheel, wheels
debt, debts	wisp, wisps
field, fields	yacht, yachts

American difference − Color(s) for colour(s).

Less straightforward plurals are covered in the following sub-sections of this chapter.

✔ Checkpoints 1

In 1 to 5 below, which of the words *in italics* are spelt correctly and which incorrectly?

1 *Arrivalls* at *airports* form long *files* at *entrancs* to Customs.

2 They arrived by *parachuts* or *balloons*, as quietly as *ghostes* or *wisps*.

3 Several *circuits* of the *fields* later the *joggers* were in the bar seeking *antidots* for their tiredness.

4 The *microcomputers* processed to the *printers* the *receiptes* for *purchases* of *magazins* and *books*.

5 *Managers* at each of the *centrs* were responsible for checking *spectators* coming through the *turnstils*.

See page 228 for Checkpoint Checks

2. Plurals of words ending in y

If there is a vowel immediately before the **y**, adding an **s** is the basic rule for forming the plural. Thus:

alley, alleys (paths)
alloy, alloys
attorney, attorneys
bogey, bogeys (in golf)
boy, boys
byway, byways
chimney, chimneys
delay, delays
donkey, donkeys
envoy, envoys
galley, galleys
journey, journeys
key, keys
lackey, lackeys

monkey, monkeys
play, plays
ploy, ploys
spray, sprays
storey, storeys
stray, strays
subway, subways
survey, surveys
tray, trays
trolley, trolleys
underlay, underlays
valley, valleys
volley, volleys

If there is a consonant immediately before the **y**, a different rule applies. The **y** becomes **ies**. For example:

ally, allies (friends)
baby, babies
beauty, beauties
body, bodies
bogy, bogies (ghosts)
curry, curries
eighty, eighties
enemy, enemies
enquiry, enquiries
family, families
fly, flies
gantry, gantries
inquiry, inquiries
jalopy, jalopies

lady, ladies
lorry, lorries
ministry, ministries
monastery, monasteries
opportunity, opportunities
pony, ponies
pygmy, pygmies
responsibility, responsibilities
ruby, rubies
sky, skies
story, stories
tendency, tendencies
tragedy, tragedies

Note: Ally (meaning friend) is unusual in the list immediately above in that the **y** is pronounced as **eye** instead of **ee**. It should not, of course, be confused with alley/alleys (footpath(s)) in the preceding list.

Pygmy/pygmies can also be pigmy/pigmies.

Exceptions:

i)   Proper nouns ending in **y** preceded by a consonant simply add an **s** rather than converting to **ies** — *as in 'the Jollys have gone on holiday' or 'the Parrys are moving house'*.

ii)   The horse-drawn carriage known as a fly becomes flys (unlike the insect, which becomes flies).

Checkpoints 2

In each of the group of four words in 1 to 5 below, two are misspelt.
Which?

| 1 | galleys | ministrys |
| | chimnies | underlays |

| 2 | gantrys | attornies |
| | envoys | plays |

| 3 | alloies | boys |
| | ninetys | skies |

| 4 | bodys | donkies |
| | stories | rubies |

| 5 | families | ploys |
| | subwayes | lackies |

In 6 to 10 below, which of the words *in italics* are correct and which
incorrect? Correct the latter.

6 Wandering the *byways* on his *ponys* he made a few *enemies*, but not
   usually among the *ladys*.

7 *Volleys* of gunfire echoed through the *vallies* from the direction of
   the *monasterys*.

8 The raging *beautys* ate their *curries* and flashed their *rubies* while
   dressed more for the naughty *ninetys* than the moderate *eighties*.

9 Together, the *allys* crept through the *alleys* and *bywaies* making
   surveys of their *enemys*.

10 The *trollies* were handy for carrying the *trays*, except on *lorrys* or
    between *storeys*.

See page 228 for Checkpoint Checks

3. Plurals of words ending in -ch, -tch, s, sh, ss, x or z

If a word has one of the above endings in the singular, it normally adds **-es** to form the plural. For example:

bench, benches	lunch, lunches
bunch, bunches	porch, porches
church, churches	torch, torches
crunch, crunches	trench, trenches
hunch, hunches	
crutch, crutches	hutch, hutches
despatch, despatches	
bus, buses	hiatus, hiatuses
census, censuses	
brush, brushes	flush, flushes
bush, bushes	mackintosh, mackintoshes
crash, crashes	rush, rushes
crush, crushes	varnish, varnishes
dash, dashes	
ass, asses	cross, crosses
brass, brasses	harness, harnesses
canvass, canvasses	pass, passes
(*meaning seeking votes*)	premiss, premisses[1]
carcass, carcasses	witness, witnesses
fix, fixes	thorax, thoraxes
fox, foxes	
waltz, waltzes	

[1]Premiss, meaning basis for a statement, should not be confused with premise, meaning a building, the plural of which is straightforwardly premises, as in **8.1** above.

Exceptions:

i)   Canvas, meaning a strong, heavy cloth or a boat-end, can become either canvases or canvasses in the plural. Neither should be confused with canvasses, the plural of canvas, meaning seeking votes.

ii)   Some **s** ending words — for example, axis and basis — do not follow the above rule but are among words of foreign origin in **8.9** below.

✓ Checkpoints 3

In 1 to 5, which are the correct spellings?

1   (a) varnishes or varnishs?
     (b) buses or busses?
     (c) bushs or bushes?

2   (a) canvasses or canvases
     (b) harneses or harnesses?
     (c) foxes or foxs?

3   (a) benchs or benches?
     (b) churches or churchs?
     (c) mackintoshs or mackintoshes?

4   (a) hutches or hutchs?
     (b) pases or passes?
     (c) hiatusses or hiatuses?

5   (a) crutchs or crutches?
     (b) despatches or despaches?
     (c) mackintoshs or mackintoshes?

See page 229 for Checkpoint Checks

4. Plurals of -f or -fe endings

Some words ending in **-f** just add **s** to form their plurals. For example:

chief, chiefs	oaf, oafs	staff, staffs
cliff, cliffs	roof, roofs	tiff, tiffs
muff, muffs	skiff, skiffs	toff, toffs

There are other words ending in **-f** or **-fe** that change their endings to **-ves** in the plural. They include:

calf, calves	life, lives	thief, thieves
half, halves	loaf, loaves	wife, wives
knife, knives	sheaf, sheaves	wolf, wolves
leaf, leaves	shelf, shelves	yourself, yourselves

With a few words, either **-fs** or **-ves** is an acceptable ending for their plurals. Thus:

dwarf	dwarfs or dwarves
handkerchief	handkerchiefs or handkerchieves
hoof	hoofs or hooves
scarf	scarfs or scarves
turf	turfs or turves
wharf	wharfs or wharves

✓ Checkpoints 4

Which are the correct plurals in 1 to 5 below?

1 (a) knife – knives or knifes?
   (b) hoof – hoofs or hooves?
   (c) wolf – wolfs or wolves?

2 (a) chief – chiefs or chieves?
   (b) roof – rooves or roofs?
   (c) shelf – shelfs or shelves?

3 (a) turf – turfs or turves?
   (b) wife – wives or wifes?
   (c) scarf – scarfs or scarves?

4 (a) thief – thiefs or thieves?
   (b) loaf – loafs or loaves?
   (c) dwarf – dwarfs or dwarves?

5 (a) life – lifes or lives?
   (b) self – selfs or selves?
   (c) handkerchief –
       handkerchiefs or
       handkerchieves?

See page 229 for Checkpoint Checks

5. Plurals of -o endings

If an **-o** ending is preceded by a vowel, this usually a case for forming the plural by simply adding an **s**. For example:

audio, audios	punctilio, punctilios
cameo, cameos	radio, radios
cuckoo, cuckoos	ratio, ratios
curio, curios	scenario, scenarios
impresario, impresarios	stereo, stereos
oratorio, oratorios	video, videos

Where an **-o** ending is preceded by a consonant, some words add **s** only to form plurals, others add **es**. There is no rule that helps distinguish between the two groups.

The following words have **s** only added:

albinos	dynamos	kilos	placebos
altos	egos	lassos[1]	pros
archipelagos	embryos	librettos	provisos
armadillos	Eskimos	magnetos	solos
banjos	fiascos	manifestos[1]	sopranos
boleros	flamingos[1]	memos	stilettos
bravos	frescos[1]	micros	tiros (tyros)
commandos	gauchos	photos	tobaccos
concertos	ghettos[1]	pianos	torsos
crescendos	gringos	piccolos	zeros[1]

[1]Some dictionaries also allow **-es** endings for these words.

Words ending with **-o** preceded by a consonant that usually form their plurals by adding **-es** include:

buffaloes[2]	haloes[1]	negroes	tornadoes[1]
calicoes[1]	heroes	noes[1]	torpedoes
cargoes[1]	innuendoes[1]	peccadilloes[1]	vetoes
dominoes	mangoes[1]	porticoes[1]	volcanoes[1]
echoes	mementoes	potatoes	
embargoes	mosquitoes	salvoes[1]	
grottoes[1]	mottoes[1]	tomatoes	

¹But straight **s** endings, without **e**, are also just about acceptable for these words.

²Buffalo can be both singular and plural.

 Checkpoints 5

In 1 to 10 below, in each group of four words which are spelt correctly and which incorrectly?

1	cameoes	cuckoos
	audios	stereoes
2	curios	ratios
	videoes	fiascoes
3	dynamos	egos
	cargos	mottos
4	scenarioes	lassos
	gringos	gauchos
5	crescendoes	provisos
	oratorioes	Eskimos
6	negroes	zeroes
	microes	embargoes
7	tobaccos	mosquitos
	soloes	radios
8	dominos	impresarios
	buffalos	sopranos
9	torsoes	haloes
	heroes	stilettoes
10	echoes	mementoes
	mangos	vetos

See page 230 for Checkpoint Checks

6. Plurals by vowel change

A few words form plurals largely by changes in the middle rather than the ending. Thus:

foot − feet　　　　louse − lice　　　　tooth − teeth
goose − geese　　　man − men　　　　woman − women

✓ Checkpoints 6

In 1 and 2, are the words *in italics* spelt correctly?

1　*Men* putting their best *feet* forward make more impact than *women* nobly gritting their *teeth*.

2　These *geese* are not normally affected by *louce*.

See page 230 for Checkpoint Checks

7. No change between plural and singular

There are some words that make no change between plural and singular either (a) because their plurals are the same as their singulars, (b) because they appear in the plural only, or (c) because they are plurals but treated as singulars.

a) Words that are the same in the plural as in the singular include:

aircraft	deer	grouse	pike	series	species
cod	fish	know-how	salmon	sheep	swine

b) Words or nouns that appear in the plural only include:

cattle	forceps	pincers	pliers	scissors	shears

c) Nouns that may look like plurals at first sight but should be treated as singulars include:

athletics	gymnastics	mathematics
economics	logistics	politics

✓ Checkpoints 7

Which, in 1 to 3, are the correct plurals?

1. (a) fish or fishes?
   (b) cod or cods?
   (c) chip or chips?

2. (a) grouse or grouses?
   (b) sheep or sheeps?
   (c) species or speciess?

3. (a) salmon or salmons?
   (b) cattle or cattles?
   (c) cow or cows?

Which of the verbs *in italics* in 4 and 5 are used correctly?

4   Forceps *are* used by surgeons, pliers *is* used by electricians, scissors
     is used by dressmakers, while shears *are* put to good use by
     gardeners.

5   Economics, like mathematics, *is* a popular academic subject,
     athletics *are* a welcome outdoor recreation, gymnastics *are* an
     indoor recreation, while politics, some would say, *are* a mirror to
     life.

See page 231 for Checkpoint Checks

8. Plurals of compound or hyphenated words

Broadly speaking, in hyphenated words forming compound nouns, the plural ending (usually **-s**) is given to the most important word. For example:

court-martial, courts-martial
lady-in-waiting, ladies-in-waiting
looker-on, lookers-on
man-of-war, men-of-war
mother-in-law, mothers-in-law
passer-by, passers-by

In the above cases, the key or important words are obviously court, lady, looker, man, mother, passer, so they take the plurals.

But if man or woman is the first part of a compound word consisting of two nouns, both parts of the word take the plural:

woman-worker, women-workers   man-Friday, men-Fridays

Most commonly, however, it is the last part of a compound noun that takes the plural, whether it consists of, for instance, two nouns (eg birth-rate/birth-rates), an adjective or adverb and noun (eg back-bencher(s) or by-road(s)), or a verb and adverb (eg change-over(s)). For example:

air-blasts	ear-rings	major-generals
back-benchers	filter-papers	micro-computers
birth-rates	hand-outs	micro-organisms
by-elections	head-dresses	notice-boards
by-laws	heart-breaks	pocket-books
by-products	hip-joints	post-mortems
by-roads	jaw-bones	rate-payers
change-overs	kick-offs	record-players
corner-stones	knick-knacks	sea-breezes
cross-references	lay-bys	set-backs
cross-sections	lay-offs	take-offs
death-rates	line-outs	take-overs
die-hards	looking-glasses	turning-points
ding-dongs	look-outs	wage-earners

Some of the above hyphenated or compound words are sometimes merged into a single word (eg handouts, microcomputers or ratepayers), while others are sometimes used as separate words without a hyphen (eg filter papers, pocket books or record players). If either of these alternatives is a possibility, this is an indication that it is the end part that takes the plural.

Checkpoints 8

In 1 to 5 below, which of the compound or hyphenated words *in italics* are spelt correctly and which incorrectly?

1   *Court-martials* are among the few occasions *Majors-General* can hope to win *dings-dong* with *mothers-in-law*.

2   *Looker-ons* and *passers-by* were impressed by the sight of the *lady-in-waitings* boarding the *men-of-war*.

3   *By-products* of *by- elections* can be *heart-breaks* or *sets-back* for the ruling party or *takes-over* by the opposition and *change-overs* in Parliament among the *back-benchers*.

4   *Micro-computers*, *notice-boards* and *hand-outs* are means of communication with *cross-sections* of *wage-earners*.

5   The sounds of the *record-players* of the *woman-workers* were wafted along by the *sea-breezes* to the *looks-out* on the beach.

See page 231 for Checkpoint Checks

9. Plurals of words of foreign origin

A number of words of foreign origin − mainly Latin or French − have special plural forms. There are others − foreign-influenced or anglicised − that have alternative plurals.

Words of foreign origin with special plural forms include:

addendum, addenda
aficionado, aficionados
alumnus, alumni
alumna, alumnae
analysis, analyses
antenna, antennae[1]
antithesis, antitheses
axis, axes
basis, bases
chateau, chateaux
corrigendum, corrigenda
crisis, crises
criterion, criteria
datum, data

desideratum, desiderata
erratum, errata
hypothesis, hypotheses
iris, irises
maximum, maxima
metamorphosis, metamorphoses
minimum, minima
oasis, oases
parenthesis, parentheses
phenomenon, phenomena
stimulus, stimuli
synopsis, synopses
thesis, theses

[1]For insects only; for aerials only the plural is antennas.

Words with a choice of foreign-influenced and anglicised plurals include:

alkali, alkalis or alkalies
apex, apexes or apices
appendix, appendices or appendixes
bureau, bureaux or bureaus
cactus, cacti or cactuses
calculus, calculi or calculuses
concerto, concerti or concertos
crematorium, crematoria or crematoriums
crocus, croci or crocuses
crux, cruces or cruxes
curriculum, curricula or curriculums
dilettante, dilettanti or dilettantes

focus, foci or focuses
formula, formulae or formulas
fungus, fungi or funguses
genius, genii or geniuses[1]
gladiolus, gladioli or gladioluses
gymnasium, gymnasia or gymnasiums
helix, helices or helixes
index, indices or indexes[1]
larva, larvae or larvas
maestro, maestri or maestros
matrix, matrices or matrixes
mausoleum, mausolea or mausoleums
medium, media or mediums[1]
memorandum, memoranda or memorandums
nucleus, nuclei or nucleuses
plateau, plateaux or plateaus
radius, radii or radiuses
referendum, referenda or referendums
sanatorium, sanatoria or sanatoriums
spectrum, spectra or spectrums
stratum, strata or stratums
syllabus, syllabi or syllabuses
tableau, tableaux or tableaus
terminus, termini or terminuses
virtuoso, virtuosi or virtuosos
vortex, vortices or vortexes

Note: [1]There is a distinction of meaning in the plurals of these words. 'Geniuses' is the usual plural of 'genius', while 'genii' is often reserved for 'genie.' The plural of 'index' is commonly 'indexes' but 'indices' in the mathematical sense. The plural of 'medium' is normally 'mediums', but 'media' is used for the Press, TV etc.

☑ Checkpoints 9

In 1 to 5 below, which of the plurals *in italics* are spelt correctly and which incorrectly?

1   Strange *phenomenons* would be at work if *oases* appeared as mirages on *plateaux*.

2   Unknown *viruses* had created the *crisises* that led to pressure on space in the *sanatoria* but not, fortunately, the *mausoleums*.

3   The grounds of the *chateaus* were wild with *cacti*, *fungi*, *crocuses* and *gladioli*.

4   *Analyses* of *data* on the careers of *alumnuses* supported their *hypotheses* that the right *criterions* had been established for the *curriculums* and *syllabi*.

5   The *dilettanti* among the *maestros* issued numerous *addendums*, *corrigendums* and *errata* challenging the *bases* of the *formulae* in the *memoranda* and the *appendices*.

See page 232 for Checkpoint Checks

10. Irregular plurals

A small number of nouns take their plurals irregularly, in ways
peculiar to themselves. They include:

child, children	man, men	ox, oxen	woman, women
louse, lice	mouse, mice	penny, pence	

9. Sound-alike or confusing word beginnings and prefixes

Sound-alike or otherwise confusing word beginnings or prefixes considered in this chapter are

1. **ante-** or **anti-**
2. **en-**, **in-**, **em-** or **im-**
3. **un-**, **in-**, **il-**, **im-** or **ir-** as negative prefixes
4. **for-** or **fore -**.

1. ante- or anti-

A clear and relatively reliable indicator is the difference in meaning between **ante-** (from the Latin meaning 'before') and **anti-** (from the Greek for 'opposed to' or 'opposite').

ante- examples are:

antecedent	antedate	antenatal	antepost
antechamber	antediluvian	antenuptial	anterior
antechapel	ante meridiem	antepenultimate	anteroom

Note: i) Some of the above examples are sometimes spelt with a hyphen (eg ante-post and ante-room).

ii) An unusual example of the prefix remaining separate is ante meridiem (am or before noon).

iii) Words that are prefixed **ante-** but have no connection with the 'before' meaning are antelope and antenna.

anti- examples (one or two hyphenated) are:

anti-aircraft	antifreeze	antipodes
antiballistic	antigen	antipole
antibiotic	antihero	antipope
antibody	antihistamine	antiseptic
antichrist	antiknock	antiserum
anticlerical	antilogarithm	antisocial
anticlimax	antimacassar	antitank
anticlockwise	anti-novel	antithesis
anticoagulant	antipathetic	antitoxin
anticyclone	antipathy	antitrust
antidepressant	antipersonnel	antivivisection
antidote	antiperspirant	

Note: i) Words beginning with **anti-** which do not have an opposite or opposed meaning include: anticipate; antics; antiquarian; antique.

ii) Some of the above are sometimes spelt with a hyphen − for example, anti-hero and anti-personnel.

iii) A word sometimes confused as to **ante-** or **anti-** is antonym.

2. en-, in-, em- or im-

Often, again, pronunciation is a sound test for distinguishing between these prefixes, but examples where confusion sometimes persists include the **en-** words below:

enable	endure	enrich	entrails
enact	energise	enrol[1]	entrain
enamour	energy	ensconce	entrance
encamp	enervate	enshrine	entrap
encapsulate	enfeeble	enshroud	entreat
enchain	enfold	ensign	entrée
enchant	enforce	enslave	entrench
encircle	enfranchise	ensnare	entwine
enclave	engage	ensue	enumerate
enclose	engender	ensure[1]	enunciate
encompass	engine	entail	envelop
encounter	engrave	entangle	*(the verb)*
encourage	engross	enterprise	envelope
encroach	engulf	entertain	*(the noun)*
encrust	enhance	enthral[1]	envious
encumber	enigma	enthrone	environment
encyclical	enjoin	enthusiasm	environs
endanger	enjoy	entice	envisage
endear	enlarge	entitle	envoy
endeavour	enlist	entity	envy
endemic	enliven	entomb	enzyme
endive	enmesh	entomology	
endow	enrage	entourage	

Note: i) The pronunciation test works for most of the above words and most others with an **en-** prefix. Most often, the pronunciation of **en-** is as in 'hen' or 'enable', but occasionally can be [ahn] as in entourage or entrée (both borrowed from the French with or without the acute accent) or the way some people pronounce envelope.

ii) [1]*American difference* — endeavor for endeavour; enroll for enrol; insure for ensure; enthrall for enthral.

The pronunciation test works even more clearly for **in-** prefixes. Many words in the English language begin with **in-**, so only a few examples are given below. First are some that are confused on occasion with **en-**. Then, later in this chapter, there are some adjectives and adverbs with negative **in-** prefixes that are sometimes confused with **un-** prefixes.

inaugurate	indictment	innuendo	interval
incarcerate	indignity	inquest	intonation
incense	indolent	insinuate	introvert
incentive	induct	insomnia	intrude
inception	indulge	install[1]	intuition
income	infancy	instalment[1]	inundate
incorporate	infinitive	instil[1]	invective
incrustation	ingrained	intelligence	inventory
incur	ingratiate	intend	invocation
incurred	initiate	interchange	invoke
indent	inland	interface	invoice
indicate	innovate	interleave	involve

[1]American difference − instal for install; installment for instalment; instill for instil (see also Chapter 3, pages 27-8).

There are a few words that can have either **en-** or **in-** beginnings. They include:

encase or incase	engraft or ingraft	enquiry or inquiry
endorse or indorse	enquire or inquire	entrust or intrust

Note: i) The **en-** spelling is the more common choice with most of the above words.

ii) Enquiry and enquire are normally associated with asking a question, while inquiry and inquire are used for a formal investigation (such as a Public Inquiry).

em- beginnings include:

emaciated	emblazon	emeritus	empire
emanate	emblem	emery	empiric
emancipate	embody	emetic	emplacement
emasculate	embolden	emigrate	emplane
embalm	emboss	émigré	employ
embankment	embrace	eminence	emporium
embargo	embrocation	emit	empower
embark	embroider	emissary	empress
embarrass	embroil	emollient	empty
embassy	embryo	emolument	emu
embattled	emend	emotion	emulate
embellish	emerald	empathy	emulsion
ember	emerge	emperor	
embezzle	emergency	emphasise	

Note: Again, the pronunciation test usually helps, but the **e** may be either short (as in 'hen') or, less often, long (as in 'metre'). Examples of the short vowel are embalm, embargo, embattled, embody, emboss, emerald, emissary, emperor, emulate. Long-vowel examples are emend, emerge, emit, emu.

im- beginnings include the following. There is also the use of **im-** as a negative prefix, covered later in this chapter.

image	impact	impetuous	impound
imagine	impair	impetus	impoverish
imbecile	impale	impinge	imprecation
imbibe	impart	impish	impregnable
imbue	impasse	implacable	impresario
imitate	impassioned	implant	impress (*the verb*)
immaculate	impeach	implement	imprint
immediate	impede	implicate	imprison
immemorial	impel	implicit	impromptu
immense	impending	implore	improvise
immerse	imperial	imply	impudent
immigrant	imperil	import	impugn
imminent	imperious	important	impulse
immiscible	impersonate	importune	impunity
immolate	impertinent	impose	impute
immune	imperturbable	imposing	
immure	impetigo	impostor	

There are one or two words that can have either **em-** or **im-** beginnings. They include:

embed or imbed   empanel or impanel

Note: In both the above cases, **em-** is the more usual spelling.

3. un-, in-, il-, im- or ir- as negative prefixes

Confusion between **un-** and **in-** beginnings arises largely with
negative prefixes — that is, prefixes imparting a negative meaning
to the original word or root (for example, **un-** giving 'able' the
opposite and negative meaning of unable). There is no really firm
rule distinguishing the **un-** from **in-** except — for the classicists —
that words of Latin origin tend to take the **in-** prefix. But not
always: for example, able and ability obviously come from the
same root source, but while the former takes **un-**, the latter takes
in-.

There is then the further complication that what would otherwise
be **in-** prefixes become **il-** before **l**, **im-** before **b**, **m** or **p**, or **ir-**
before **r**.

Since there is no readily recognisable way of distinguishing
between **un-** and **in-** (short of taking a degree in classics!), some
examples of **un-** words — nearly 200 of them — are given below.

unabashed	unaware	unclean
unabated	unbalanced	uncommitted
unable (*but*	*unbearable*	*uncommon*
inability)	unbecoming	uncommunicative
unaccompanied	unbeknown	uncompromising
unaccountable	unbeliever	unconcerned
unaccustomed	unbend	unconditional
unadopted	unbiased	unconscionable
unaffected	unblushing	unconscious
unalloyed	unborn	unconsidered
unalterable	unbridled	uncouple
unannounced	unbroken	uncouth
unanswerable	unburden	uncover
unapproachable	unbutton	undaunted
unarmed	uncanny	undecided
unasked	unceasing	undeclared
unassuming	unceremonious	undefended
unattached	uncertain	undemonstrative
unattended	uncharitable	undeniable
unavailing	uncharted	undenominational
unavoidable	unchecked	undesirable

undeterred	unfrequented	unmanned
undeveloped	unfriendly	unmask
undischarged	unfrock	unmatchable
undo	unfruitful	unmeasurable
undock	unfurl	unmentionable
undoubted	unfurnished	unmindful
undreamed	ungainly	unmistakable
(or undreamt)	ungenerous	unmitigated
undress	ungodly	unmoved
undying	ungovernable	unnamed
unearned	ungrammatical	unnatural
unearthly	ungrateful	unnecessary
uneasy	unguarded	unnoticed
uneaten	unhappy	unnumbered
uneducated	unhealthy	unobtrusive
unemployed	unheard	unofficial
unending	unhinge	unorthodox
unenlightened	unholy	unpack
unequal	unhorse	unparalleled
unequivocal	unidentified	unpick
unerring	unimaginative	unplaced
unexceptionable	unimportant	unplayable
unexpected	uninhabitable	unpleasant
unfailing	uninhabited	unpractised
unfair	uninitiated	unprecedented
unfaithful	uninspired	unprejudiced
unfaltering	uninterested	unpremeditated
unfamiliar	unjust (*but*	unprepossessing
unfathomable	injustice)	unpretentious
unfeeling	unkempt	unprincipled
unfeigned	unkind	unprintable
unfit	unknowing	unprofessional
unflagging	unleash	unprofitable
unflappable	unleavened	unprompted
unflinching	unlike	unprovoked
unfold	unlimited	unqualified
unforeseen	unload	unquestionable
unforgettable	unloose	unquestioning
unfortunate	unmanageable	unravel
unfounded	unmanly	unreal

unreasonable	unreliable	unreservedly
unreasoning	unrelieved	unrest
unrehearsed	unremitting	unrestricted
unrelenting	unrequited	untold

The **in-** beginning is used as a negative prefix in a smaller number of words, including the following:

inability	inconsistent	infrequent
inaccessible	incredible	ingenious
inaccurate	incredulity	ingenuous
inactive	incurable	inglorious
inadequate	indecisive	ingratitude
inadvertent	indefatigable	inharmonious
inanimate	indefinite	inhuman
inarticulate	indelible	injustice
inattentive	indelicate	innocent
inaudible	independent	innocuous
inauspicious	indestructible	innumerate
incalculable	indigestible	insufferable
incapable	indignant	intolerable
incoherent	inedible	intolerant
incombustible	ineducable	intransigent
incomparable	inelegant	invalid
incompatible	ineligible	invariable
inconceivable	inept	invidious
inconclusive	inexact	invisible
inconsiderate	infallible	invulnerable

The **il-** negative prefix is used with the following roots beginning with **l**:

| illegal | illegitimate | illicit | illiquid | illogical |
| illegible | illiberal | illimitable | illiterate | |

The **im-** negative prefix is used with the following roots beginning with **b**, **m** or **p**:

imbalance	impartial	impolite
immaterial	impassable	impolitic
immature	impassive	imponderable
immeasurable	impatient	impossible
immobile	impenetrable	important
immobilise	imperceptible	impracticable
immobility	imperfect	impractical
immoderate	imperishable	improbable
immodest	impermanent	improper
immoral	impermeable	improvident
immortal	impersonal	imprudent
immovable	impervious	impure
immutable	impiety	
impalpable	impious	

The **ir-** negative prefix is used with roots beginning with **r**, though that is not to say that all such roots take an **ir-** prefix. A number that do not have already been noted (eg unreasonable, unrelenting, unrestricted). Words that do take **ir-** include:

irrational	irreligious	irresolvable
irreclaimable	irremediable	irrespective
irreconcilable	irremovable	irresponsible
irrecoverable	irreparable	irretrievable
irredeemable	irreplaceable	irreverent
irreducible	irrepressible	irreversible
irrefutable	irreproachable	irrevocable
irregular	irresistible	
irrelevant	irresolute	

4. for- or fore-

When is **for-** the correct prefix and when **fore-**? Fortunately, there are few enough of both kinds of words to become familiar with most of them individually. However, if you would like general rules to help you, the following might be useful.

According to *Fowler's Modern English Usage*, **for-** usually imparts a meaning of 'away, out, completely'; or implies 'prohibition or abstention'. The **fore-** prefix, on the other hand, often imparts a sense of being in the forefront or looking to the future.

for- prefixes include:

forage	forborne	forgive	forswear
foray	forceful	forgo (do without)	forsworn
forbad(e)	forcible	forgotten	forward
forbear[1]	forfeit	forlorn	
forbid	forgather[2]	formidable	
forbidden	forget	forsake	

fore- prefixes include:

forearm	forehand	foresail
forebear[1]	forehead	foresee
foreboding	foreign[3]	foreshadow
forecast	foreknow	foreshore
forecastle	foreland	foreshorten
foreclose	foreleg	foreseen
forecourt	forelimb	foresight
forefather	forelock	forestall
forefeel	foreman	foretaste
forefinger	foremast	foretell
forefoot	foremost	forethought
forefront	forenoon	foretoken
foregather[2]	foreordain	foretop
forego (precede)	forepaw	forewarn
foreground	forerunner	foreword

[1]For the verb meaning to abstain or restrain, forbear is the correct spelling. For the noun meaning ancestor, either forbear or forebear is correct.

[2]Forgather and foregather are alternative spellings.

[3]Foreign is in a sense the odd one out in the above list, the **e** in it forming a diphthong with the following **i**.

Checkpoints

In 1 to 12 below, in each group of four words which two are spelt
correctly and which incorrectly? Correct the latter.

1   anticedent   anticyclone
    anteclimax   antisocial

2   antenatal   antichamber
    antifreeze   antiroom

3   antediluvian   antecoagulant
    incroach   ensnare

4   enable   infold
    intangle   encircle

5   envolve   initiate
    endictment   engender

6   imbattled   imbellish
    impair   impede

7   embankment   implant
    imerge   emmaculate

8   emmense   embassy
    empetigo   impulse

9   inable   unability
    unhealthy   unrest

10 impassive   inmunity
    initerate   irreverent

11 forelorn   forarm
    forsake   forecourt

12 inpugn   impoverish
    forsail   forcible

In 13 to 20, which of the words *in italics* are spelt correctly and which
incorrectly? Correct the latter.

13 *Antedotes* to the sound of *anti-aircraft* missiles, *antetank* guns and
    antipersonnel weapons include *embarking* for the *antipodes*.

14 The *antiroom* to the surgery held stocks of *antidepressants*, *antebiotics*, *antiperspirants* and *anteseptics* fit for *antiheroes*.

15 Adding *antefreeze* to the *engine* seemed to *ingender* an immediate need for an *antiknock* additive to *insure* quieter running.

16 The *inclosed* area enabled them to muffle the *impact* without *emitting* too much noise and causing *imbarrassment*.

17 Whether *embedded* in the superstructure or *emcrusted* on it, the debris was an *innecessary* hazard though *imperceptible* at a distance.

18 The *unreliability* of the car and its *unability* to start *indeniably* explained why he was *unable* to arrive on time in spite of the *invective* he *injustly* heaped on it.

19 It was the *inpartial* opinion of the *imissary* from the *embassy* that to be *forewarned* was to be *forarmed*.

20 Weather *forcasters' forays* into the unknown *foretoken* general *forebodings* rather than accurate *forwarnings*.

In 21 to 27, which are the correct spellings?

21 (a) antidate or antedate?
   (b) antipathy or antepathy?
   (c) antipenultimate or antepenultimate?

22 (a) incourage or encourage?
   (b) endemic or emdemic?
   (c) ensure or insure?

23 (a) indictment or endictment?
   (b) emaciated or imaciated?
   (c) unflagging or inflagging?

24 (a) inplacable or implacable?
   (b) inperceptible or imperceptible?
   (c) improvident or unprovident?

25 (a) illicit or irlicit?
   (b) invocation or imvocation?
   (c) forcible or forcible?

26 (a) forword or foreword?
   (b) forehand or forhand?
   (c) forehead or forhead?

27 (a) forefather or forfather?
   (b) unresponsible or irresponsible?
   (c) forerunner or forrunner?

In 28 to 35, what are the missing letters?

28 (a) ant_rior   (b) ant_clockwise
     (c) ant_cyclone   (d) ant_podes

29 (a) _nslave   (b) _ntrovert
     (c) i_mortal   (d) _ncoherent

30 (a) _nrest   (b) _ncounter
     (c) _ngratiate   (d) i_minent

31 (a) i_regular   (b) _ntonation
     (c) i_munity   (d) _mergency

32 (a) i_undate   (b) _nquest
     (c) _nlimited   (d) _ncase

33 (a) _nfortunate   (b) i_personate
     (c) _motion   (d) _ndure

34 (a) i_licit   (b) _nerring
     (c) i_literate   (d) i_resolute

35 (a) _mbalm   (b) _nsipid
     (c) _nnocuous   (d) _nconcerned

See page 233 for Checkpoint Checks

10. Silent word beginnings, and some silent middles

Confusion can sometimes be caused where a word has an initial letter that is silent. In some cases, too, a silent letter can appear in the middle of a word.

1. Silent initial letter

The most frequently used silent letter is probably **h**, as in:

haute-cuisine[1]	heirloom	honorary	hostler
hauteur[1]	honest	honour[2]	hour
heir	honorand	honourable[2]	hourly
heiress	honorarium	hors d'œuvre	

[1] French extraction is the reason for the silent **h**.

[2] *American difference* − honor for honour and, similarly, honorable for honourable.

There is also the occasional silent **a**, as in: aisle

Common examples of silent initial letters are **g, k, p** and **w**. For example:

gnarled	gnathic	gnomic	gnostic
gnash	gnaw	gnomon	gnu
gnat	gnome		

knack	knell	knighthood	know
knapweed	knew	knitting	knowledge
knapsack	knickerbockers	knob	knuckle
knave	knickers	knock	knurl
knead	knickknack¹	knockout	
knee	knife	knoll	
kneel	knight	knot	

¹Example of silent letter in middle of word in addition to the silent initial letter.

pneumatic	pseud	psychoanalysis	ptarmigan
pneumaticity	pseudonym	psychogenic	pterodactyl
pneumoconiosis	psoriasis	psychology	Ptolemy
pneumonia	psyche	psychopath	ptomaine
psalm	psychedelic	psychosis	
psalter	psychiatry	psychosomatic	
psephology	psychic	psychotherapy	

whore	wreak	wrestle	writ
wrack	wreath (noun)	wretch	write
wraith	wreathe (verb)	wrick (or rick)	writhe
wrangle	wreck	wriggle	written
wrangler	wreckage	wright	wrong
wrap	wrecker	wring	wrongly
wrapper	wren	wrinkle	wrought
wrath	wrench	wrist	wry
wrathful	wrest	wristwatch	

2. Silent middle letters

Examples of silent letters in mid-word include the following:

Silent **e**:

   bludgeon, curmudgeon, dungeon, luncheon, omelette, pigeon, sturgeon, surgeon.

Silent **g**:

   campaign, foreign, poignant, reign.

Silent **k**:

   unknowing, unknown (and similar cases where the silent middle letter is in effect the initial letter of the root covered earlier in this chapter).

Silent **u**:

   biscuit, buoy, buoyant, honour[1], labour[1], mould[1], moulder[1], moult[1], savour[1], smoulder[1].

   [1]*American difference* – the **u** is dropped (eg labor, smolder)

Silent **w**:

   answer, playwright, sword, wheelwright.

Checkpoints

Which are the missing silent letters in 1 to 8 below?

1 (a) _nockers   (b) _nome
   (c) ans_er   (d) _neumonia

2 (a) _sychoanalysis (b) _nuckle
   (c) _eirloom   (d) _nash

3 (a) surg_on   (b) _nee
   (c) _ourly   (d) labo_r

4 (a) campai_n   (b) b_oyant
   (c) bisc_it   (d) _rap

5 (a) _rangler   (b) poi_nant
   (c) mo_lder   (d) play_right

6 (a) _reckage   (b) _naw
   (c) _salm   (d) _onest

7 (a) _nell   (b) _neumatic
   (c) bludg_on   (d) _terodactyl

8 (a) _night   (b) _nu
   (c) s_ord   (d) _rit

See page 236 for Checkpoint Checks

11. Which diphthong or digraph?

Diphthong has been defined in Chapter 1 as two vowels pronounced together in a single sound, and digraph as any two letters (vowel or consonant) pronounced in a single sound. (Thus, a digraph is also a diphthong, but not necessarily vice versa.)

Two of the most common and variously used diphthongs, **ie** and **ei**, are covered in some detail in Chapter 2, to which there are several cross-references below.

1. [ay] sound, similar to long [a] (as in sane)

use of **ei**:

beige, eight, freight, heir, reign, rein, weight

(see also Chapter 2, page 17)

use of **ae**:

Gaelic

use of **ai**

chain	frail	laid	rail	slain	trail
claim	gaiety	mail	rain	snail	train
contain	gain	main	reclaim	sprain	travail
dainty	gainful	pail (bucket)	refrain	strain	twain
fail	grain	proclaim	sail	terrain	wait

use of **ay**

array	clay	delay	fray	player	slay
bay	crayon	disarray	hooray	pray(er)	spray
bayonet	day	foray	play	relay	tray

use of **ey**:

| convey | fey | heyday | osprey | purvey | they |
| disobey | grey[1] | obey | prey (bird of) | survey | whey |

[1]*American difference* – gray for grey

2. [air] sound

use of **ea**:

bear, pear (the fruit), tear (as in hole), wear (as clothes).

use of **ai**:

air, chair, fair, hair, pair (two), stairs

3. [ar] sound (as in scar)

use of **ar**:

bar	card	disembark	hark	parley	smart
bard	carp	embark	large	park	snarl
barter	cart	garter	lark	part	starter
car	dark	hard	<u>march</u>	remark	tart

use of **er**

clerk, Derby

use of **ear**

hearth

4. [aw] sound (as in awful)

use of **al**

balk	call	fall	recall	talk	walk
ball	chalk	hall	stall	tall	wall

use of **au**

caught daughter distraught naughty slaughter taught

use of **aw**:

awesome	claw	drawing	law	pawn	spawn
brawl	coleslaw	fawn	lawyer	prawn	withdrawing
brawling	dawn	fawning	lawn	sawn	withdrawn
brawn	dawning	flaw	paw	shawl	yawn

5. [ee] sound

use of **ie**

achieve	brief	grief	piece	reprieve	siege
belief	field	niece	relief	shield	yield

(see also Chapter 2, page 16)

use of **ei**

ceiling conceive protein receipt seize   weird

(see also Chapter 2, page 17)

use of **ae**

aegis	aesthetic	encyclopaedia[1]	palaeography[1]
aeolian[1]	aestival[1]	faeces[1]	palaeolithic[1]
aeon[1]	aetiology[1]	gynaecology[1]	palaeontology[1]
Aesop	archaeology[1]	mediaeval[1]	
aesthete	Caesar	paediatrics[1]	

[1]*American differences* – **e** instead of **ae**, as an alternative also acceptable – and in some case preferred – in British English.

use of **ea**

leap, plead, real(istic), reap

use of **ee**

creed	green	reel (wind in)	spleen	three	tweed
free	preen	scree	spree	tree	weed
greed	reed (plant)	screen	teenager	tureen	

use of **oe**

diarrhoea, foetus (*American difference* − **e** for **oe**)

6. [eer] or [ere] sound, as in cheers

use of **ear**

appear, dear, disappear, ear, endear, hear (listen), near, spear

use of **eer**

beer, career, cheer, domineer, queer, seer, steer, volunteer

7. [eh] sound, similar to short [e] (as in bend)

use of **ae**

praesidium (or presidium)

use of **ie** and **ei**

friend, lieutenant (British pronunciation), leisure.

(see also Chapter 2, page 18)

use of **ea**

bread	death	health	pheasant	retread	tread
breath	endeavour	healthy	pleasant	stealth	wealth
breathless	head	peasant	pleasantry	stealthy	wealthy

8. [er] sound

use of **ear**

dearth	earn	earth	learn	search	yearn

use of **er**

berk	certificate	diverge	mercy	merge	verse
berth	converge	jerk	merge	traverse	

(*there are also the* -er *endings in Chapter 12, page 126*)

use of **ir**

bird	dirt	first	girdle	mirth	thirst
birth	fir (tree)	flirt	girth	third	whirl

use of **or** (following **w**)

word	work	world	worm	worse	worth

use of **our**

courteous	courtesy	journal	journalist	journey	scourge

use of **ur**

burble	burn	curb	furnish	lurch	purr
burden	church	curve	hurdle	murder	purse
burger	churn	furl	hurt	nurse	turkey

use of **yr**

martyr	myrrh	myrtle

9. short [i] sound (as in pin)

use of **ie**

handkerchief	mischief	series	sieve

(*see also Chapter 2, page 17*)

use of **ei**

counterfeit   foreign   forfeit   sovereign   surfeit

(see also Chapter 2, page 17)

use of **ui**

building   guild   guillotine   guinea
biscuit   guilder   guilt   guitar

*(the **ui** diphthong, of course, could also be regarded as a case of a silent [u], as in Chapter 10)*

10. long [i] sound (as in pine)

use of **ie**

die   hierarchy hieroglyphics   lie   tie

(see also Chapter 2, page 18)

use of **ei**

eiderdown either   Fahrenheit height   neither   sleight

11. short [o] sound (as in body)

use of **au**

Australia Austria   because   cauliflower   laurel   sausage

use of **ou**

cough, trough

use of **ow**

knowledge

use of **ach**

yacht

12. [oh] or long [o] sound (as in lone)

use of **oa**

boast	coach	coax	oak	road	soap
boat	coal	croak	oast	roam	toad
boater	coast	groan	oath	roast	toadstool
broach	coat	groats	oats	soak	toast

use of **oe**

doe	foe	hoe	sloe	toe	woe

use of **ow**

barrow	bungalow	furrow	snow	swallow	tow
blow	flow	mow	sparrow	tomorrow	yellow

use of **ou**

boulder	mould[1]	moult[1]	shoulder	soul	though

[1]*American difference – **o** for **ou**.*

use of **au**

mauve

use of **oo**

brooch (jewellery)

use of **ew**

sew

use of **eau**

beau, gateau (and other such words borrowed from the French)

13. [oo] sound, similar to long [u] (as in prude)

use of **ie**

(in) lieu   lieutenant[1]

[1]Pronunciation of American extraction, the [eh] pronunciation earlier in this chapter being usual in British English.

(*see also Chapter 2, page 18*)

use of **ew** (as in yew tree)

blew	brewery	crew	grew	sinew	threw
brew	cashew (nut)drew	screw	strewn	trews

use of **o**[1]

do   lose   move   remove   who   whom

[1]Not a diphthong or digraph, of course, but included here as an unusual pronunciation of **o** − neither short, as in body, nor long as in bone.

use of **oo**

bloom	brood	food	loose	mood	shoot
boom	choose	goose	loot	noodles	toot

use of **ou**

coupé	croupier	joule (of	soufflé	souvenir	toupee
croup	group	energy)	soup	through	troupe

use of **ui**

fruit   juice   recruit   suit

14. [or] sound

use of **oar**

| boar | board | hoard | hoarse | roar | soar (in air) |

use of **our**

| course | downpour | four | fourteen | mourn | pour |

15. [ow] sound

use of **ou**

| about | astound | cloud | grouse | loud | Slough |
| aloud | bough | ground | hour | round | sound |

use of **ow**

| brown | drown | frown | now | prowler | rowdy |
| clown | flower | kowtow | power | row (noise) | town |

16. [oy] sound

use of **oi**

| boil | coil | join | loiter | oil | soiled |
| choice | goitre | joinery | noise | soil | toil |

use of **oy**

| alloy | coy | joyful | loyalty | royalty | toy |
| boy | joy | loyal | royal | soya | toying |

17. [uh] sound, similar to [u] in push

use of **ie**

ancient   conscience patience   patient proficiency   proficient

(see also Chapter 2, page 18)

use of **oo**

book	cook	foot	hood	hook	wool
bookstall	cooker	good	hooded	stood	woolly

use of **ou**

could	courier	should	would

18. short [u] sound (as in run)

use of **ou**

courage	couplet	double	rough	tough	young

19. [yew] sound (similar to [ew] sound preceded by [y])

use of **ew**

askew	dewlap	few	hewn	new	pewter
dew	ewe	hew (chop)	knew	pew	steward

use of **ui**

pursuit

✔ Checkpoints

In 1 to 15 below, what are the missing digraphs or pairs of letters?

1. (a) g___ety (jollity)
   (b) terr___n
   (c) disarr___
   (d) gr___n (the colour)

2. (a) cr___on (pencil)
   (b) pl___er (of games)
   (c) hoor___ (cheer)
   (d) disob___ (go against)

3. (a) fr___l (weak)
   (b) disemb___k (leave ship)
   (c) h___rth (for fire)
   (d) cl___k (office worker)

4. (a) br___ling (fighting)
   (b) d___ghter (son's sister)
   (c) distr___ght (upset)
   (d) rel___f (sigh of)

5. (a) repr___ve
   (b) sh___ld (ought to)
   (c) ach___ve___
   (d) w___rd (strange)

6. (a) C___sar
   (b) encyclop___dia
   (c) arch___ology
   (d) f___tus

7. (a) l___yer (professional adviser)
   (b) disapp___r
   (c) t___nager (youngster)
   (d) l___utenant

8. (a) br___thless
   (b) w___lth (riches)
   (c) rec___pt
   (d) d___rth (lack)

9. (a) b___g___ (fast food)
   (b) c___tificate
   (c) m___th (jollity)
   (d) j___rnalist

10. (a) m___d___ (killing)
    (b) mart___
    (c) handkerch___f
    (d) counterf___t (false)

11. (a) g___llotine
    (b) h___rarchy
    (c) c___liflower (vegetable)
    (d) ___derdown (bed cover)

12. (a) y___ht (boat)
    (b) c___ch (carriage)
    (c) t___dst___l
    (d) sparr___ (bird)

13. (a) b___lder (large stone)
    (b) m___lder (decay)
    (c) br___ery (source of beer)
    (d) cash___ (nut)

14. (a) c___pé (car)
    (b) recr___t (newcomer)
    (c) s___r (in air)
    (d) l___ter (hang around)

15. (a) pat___nt (in hospital)
    (b) c___rier (guide, messenger)
    (c) p___ter (as in mug)
    (d) profic___nt (competent)

See page 237 for Checkpoint Checks

12. Sound-alike and confusing word endings

1. able or -ible (and -ably or -ibly and ability or ibility)

There is no simple, overriding rule to help sort out which words end in **-able** and which in **-ible**. Unless, that is, you are either a classical scholar or an etymologist – in which case, it may be helpful to know that words ending in **-able** usually have their root in the Latin ending **-abilis** or the Old French **-able**, while words ending in **-ible** go back to the Latin ending **-ibilis**.

The main rays of hope for the non-classicist are (a) you can tell **-able** is almost certainly the correct ending if there is a related word that ends in **-ate**; eg irritable and irritate; and (b) **-ible** is usual if preceded by **s** or if there is a related word ending in **ion**: eg divisible and division. However, these rules of thumb can only help with a minority of words. So it has to be mainly a case of learning the hard way or using the lists below for reference.

The rules for adding **-able** or **-ible** after a vowel are covered in Chapter 4, and those for adding them after a consonant in Chapter 5.

a) Examples of **-able** endings include:

abominable	definable	inflammable	provable
acceptable	demonstrable	inflatable	rateable
actionable	desirable	inimitable	readable
adaptable	despicable	insufferable	receivable
admirable	durable	irreconcilable	reconcilable
admittable	dutiable	irreplaceable	rectifiable
adorable	dyable	irritable	referable
advisable	eatable	justifiable	regrettable
agreeable	educable	knowledgeable	reliable
alienable	endorsable	laughable	removable
amenable	equable	likeable	reputable
amiable	evadable	liveable	retractable
appreciable	excisable	lovable	saleable
arguable	excitable	machinable	serviceable
assessable	excusable	malleable	shareable
atonable	expendable	manageable	sizeable
available	finable	manoeuvrable	solvable
avoidable	foreseeable	marriageable	storable
bearable	forgettable	measurable	suitable
believable	forgivable	movable	superannuable
blameable	gettable	nameable	tameable
bribable	giveable	noticeable	timeable
bridgeable	hireable	objectionable	tolerable
calculable	hospitable	obtainable	traceable
capable	immovable	operable	tradable
changeable	immutable	palatable	transferable
chargeable	impassable	passable	tuneable
comfortable	impeccable	payable	unconscionable
conceivable	imperturbable	peaceable	undeniable
conferrable	implacable	penetrable	unexceptionable
considerable	impressionable	perishable	unknowable
consolable	indefatigable	permeable	unmistakable
contractable	indescribable	persuadable	unshakeable
creatable	indispensable	pleasurable	usable
curable	indubitable	practicable	variable
datable	inescapable	preferable	veritable
debatable	inevitable	prescribable	
deferrable	inferable	pronounceable	

b) Examples of **-ible** endings include

accessible	discernible	incorruptible	persuasible
adducible	divisible	incredible	plausible
admissible	edible	indelible	possible
audible	eligible	indigestible	reducible
avertible	exhaustible	infallible	repressible
collapsible	expressible	intangible	reproducible
combustible	extendible	intelligible	resistible
compatible	extensible	invincible	responsible
comprehensible	fallible	irascible	reversible
contemptible	feasible	irrepressible	risible
convertible	flexible	irresistible	sensible
corruptible	forcible	legible	susceptible
credible	fusible	negligible	tangible
defensible	gullible	ostensible	visible
destructible	inaccessible	perceptible	
digestible	inaudible	perfectible	
dirigible	incorrigible	permissible	

c) **-ably** or **-ibly** and **-ability** or **ibility**

When a **-ble** ending is changed to **-bly** — usually to change an adjective into an adverb — the **-able** endings straightforwardly become **-ably**, and **-ible** becomes **-ibly**. For example:

abominably	demonstrably	irritably	suitably
admirably	desirably	laughably	tolerably
amiably	hospitably	noticeably	undeniably
arguably	impeccably	passably	unmistakably
capably	implacably	peaceably	
comfortably	indubitably	regrettably	
considerably	inevitably	reliably	

audibly	forcibly	irresistibly	responsibly
credibly	incredibly	legibly	sensibly
discernibly	indelibly	ostensibly	visibly
flexibly	irrepressibly	possibly	

Similarly, nouns ending in **-bility** take the **a** or **i** of the corresponding adjectival **-able** or **-ible**. For example:

adorability	capability	inevitability	suitability
advisability	desirability	malleability	usability
amiability	excitability	readability	variability
availability	hospitability	reliability	
accessibility	eligibility	legibility	visibility
admissibility	fallibility	permissibility	
credibility	feasibility	possibility	

✓ Checkpoints 1

In 1 to 15 below, which is the missing letter in each word, **a** or **i**?

1 (a) avail_ble   (b) blame_ble
   (c) debat_ble   (d) neglig_ble

2 (a) convert_ble   (b) admiss_ble
   (c) insuffer_ble   (d) adapt_ble

3 (a) admir_ble   (b) express_ble
   (c) ed_ble   (d) comfort_ble

4 (a) consider_ble   (b) fall_ble
   (c) respons_ble   (d) cur_ble

5 (a) manoeuvr_ble   (b) prefer_ble
   (c) suit_ble   (d) suscept_ble

6 (a) malle_ble   (b) perish_ble
   (c) destruct_ble   (d) impass_ble

7 (a) inevit_ble   (b) inimit_ble
   (c) aud_ble   (d) infall_ble

8 (a) despic_ble   (b) avoid_ble
   (c) intang_ble   (d) percept_ble

9 (a) dirig_ble   (b) divis_ble
   (c) reli_ble   (d) reput_ble

10 (a) like_ble   (b) collaps_ble
   (c) vari_ble   (d) hospit_ble

11 (a) appreci_bly   (b) desir_bility
    (c) infall_bly   (d) reli_bly

12 (a) contempt_bly   (b) like_bly
    (c) insuffer_bly   (d) unmistak_bly

13 (a) implac_bly   (b) notice_bly
    (c) indigest_bly   (d) unshake_bly

14 (a) excit_bility   (b) compat_bility
    (c) irrit_bility   (d) practic_bility

15 (a) adapt_bility   (b) elig_bility
    (c) service_bility   (d) invinc_bility

See page 238 for Checkpoint Checks

2. -ce or -se

A small number of words present a choice between **-ce** and **-se** endings. In English (as distinct from American) there are, for example, the **-ce** endings for the nouns and the **-se** for the verbs in the following:

advice − (to) advise	licence − (to) license
device − (to) devise	practice − (to) practise

Note: i) *American differences* − license (noun) for licence, practice (verb) for practise.
ii) Words derived from the above words normally take the **c** if pronounced as a hard **c**, or an **s** spelling if pronounced as either a soft **c** or a **z**. Thus:

> *hard* **c**: practicable, practical
>
> *soft* **c**: licensed, practised (*US*, practiced)
>
> **z**: advised, advisers (advisors), devised

Most other words with an ending pronounced **s** have an **-se** rather than **-ce** ending. For example:

endorse	goose	recompense
geese	mongoose	

Exceptions: ambience (being a word borrowed from the French)

A word with an ending pronounced **-ish** but taking a **-ce** spelling is: liquorice or licorice (again, a result of foreign extraction).

✓ Checkpoints 2

In 1 to 5 below, which words *in italics* are correctly spelt and which incorrectly? Correct the latter.

1. With *advisors* like those, one would be well *adviced* to look elsewhere for sound *practical advise*.

2. A *licence* is a document *deviced* to indicate who is *licenced* to *practise* the craft and who is barred by *endorsement*.

3. Having a *mongoose* as a pet is not *practisable* in this *ambiense*.

4. Feeding *geese* on *liquorice* is ill-*advised*.

5. It was some *recompense* that the *devise* indicated that the cafe was *licensed*

See page 239 for Checkpoint Checks

3. -cede, -ceed or -sede

This is a relatively easy distinction to make because only one word ends in **-sede** and three in **-ceed**. The others — though there are not many of them in total — all have **-cede** endings.

The one word ending in **-sede** is: supersede.

It has an **s** in **-sede** because its Latin root is *sedere*, to sit, while the Latin root of **-cede** and **-ceed** is *cedere*, to go or yield. Other words derived from supersede — eg superseding — also keep the **s**.

The **-cede** and **-ceed** endings are also fairly easily separated. Three basic words ending in **-ceed** are:

exceed   proceed   succeed

Some derivatives of these words retain the double **e** while others have only a single **e**. In general, the **e** remains double for a long **e** pronunciation but becomes one **e** only for a short **e** pronunciation, though there are one or two exceptions. Thus:

a) double **e**

exceeding	exceedingly	proceeding
proceedings	succeeding	

b) single **e**

excess	procedural[1]	succession	successor
excessive	success	successive	
procedure[1]	successful	successively	

[1]Single **e** although a long **e**.

Examples of the **-cede** ending are:

accede	intercede	recede
concede	precede	secede

Derivatives of these words take a single **e**, long or short, including:

acceding	interceding	precedent	seceding
accession	intercession	preceding	secession
conceding	intercessor	receding	unprecedented
concession	precedence	recession	

✔ Checkpoints 3

Which of the words *in italics* in 1 to 5 are correct and which are incorrect? Correct the latter.

1. *Proceedurally*, there was nothing to stop the front runner's *succession* if he did not *conceed* defeat himself.

2. *Succeeding* batsmen failed to *excede* the modest score of those who had *preceeded* them.

3. The possibility of *success receeded* as more and more members *seceded* from the alliance.

4. The deputy leader *succeeded* to the leadership and once more delegates *acceded* to his request for support in the election *proceedure*.

5. Central government decree can *superseed* decisions by local government, forcing *concessions* in spite of attempts to *intercede* between them.

See page 239 for Checkpoint Checks

4. -acle, -ical or -icle

-ical can be separated out from the others as an adjective ending,
not a noun. Adjectives ending in **-ical** include:

biblical	helical	musical	technological
chemical	horizontal	nautical	typical
comical	identical	physical	vertical
conical	mathematical	psychological	whimsical
critical	mechanical	radical	
farcical	medical	spherical	
geographical	methodical	technical	

The **-acle** and **-icle** endings are both for nouns only.
Pronunciation is usually a good guide to which to use.

If the ending is pronounced with an **uh**, as in buckle, the spelling is
normally **-acle**. For example:

barnacle	manacle	oracle	tentacle
coracle	miracle	pinnacle	
debacle[1]	obstacle	spectacle	

[1] **ah** rather than **uh** pronunciation, as a word borrowed from the
French.

If the ending is pronounced with an **ick**, as in sickle, the spelling is
normally **-icle**. For example:

article	cubicle	icicle	testicle
clavicle	follicle	particle	vehicle

✓ Checkpoints 4

In 1 to 5 below, which are the correct spellings?

1. (a) farcical or farcicle?
   (b) icacle or icicle?
   (c) cubicle or cubical?

2. (a) clavical or clavicle?
   (b) barnacle or barnical?
   (c) miracle or miricle?

3. (a) vehicle or vehical?
   (b) comicle or comical?
   (c) manicle or manacle?

4. (a) oracle or orical?
   (b) artical or article?
   (c) mechanicle or
       mechanical?

5. (a) methodical or
       methodacle?
   (b) obsticle or obstacle?
   (c) critical or criticle?

See page 240 for Checkpoint Checks

5. -ar, -er, -or, -re or -our

Pronunciation sometimes gives a fairly clear indication of which of these endings is correct for a particular word. Often, however, pronunciation is not a clear enough test, particularly where endings share a common [-er] sound (as in beggar, baker, author, acre, colour).

a) -ar

Words ending in **-ar** may be either adjectives or one of a small group of nouns. The adjectives (descriptive words, as defined in Chapter 1) include:

familiar	lunar	peculiar	sonar
funicular	modular	rectangular	triangular
jocular	molecular	similar	vehicular
lumbar[1]	particular	solar	

[1]Lumbar is an adjective meaning 'of the lower back region', not to be confused with lumber, noted later in this chapter, the noun meaning timber.

Nouns ending in **-ar** include:

beggar	caterpillar	grammar	vicar
burglar	cellar	scholar	
calendar (dates)	funicular	tsar (or czar)	

b) -er

The most common adjectives ending in **-er** are the comparative adjectives, such as:

better	greater	noisier	taller
bigger	hotter	smaller	
faster	larger	swifter	

There are also a few other adjectives that end in **-er**, such as:

former	proper

The **-er** nouns can be less easy to distinguish from **-or** and even **-ar** endings. Typical **-er** nouns include:

adviser[1]	discoverer	lacquer	printer
avenger	docker	launcher	producer
baker	drier	lawyer	propeller
banker	drifter	lender	protester
barter	driver	loser	publisher
bier	executioner	lumber	qualifier
blazer	exporter	(timber)	resister
bowler	farmer	maker	rider
butcher	fielder	manager	runner
buyer	fighter	manner	settler
character	flyer	master	swimmer
chopper	furnisher	mender	teacher
computer[2]	gaoler	miser	trailer
cooker	gardener	murder	winner
daughter	helicopter	organiser	worker
debater	hurdler	performer	writer
defaulter	idolater	photographer	

[1] Can also be spelt advisor. See **-er** or **-or** below for words that can have either spelling, usually in different circumstances.
[2] In the early years of 'computer' it was sometimes spelt 'computor', but the latter spelling has fallen into disuse.

c) **-or**

Nouns ending in **-or** often have Latin or Old French roots, but not obviously enough to help the spelling of non-etymologists. Nouns ending in **-or** include:

abettor	convector	emperor	prospector
advisor	councillor	erector	solicitor
author	counsellor	governor	spectator
carburettor	creator	impostor	sponsor
censor	creditor	incubator	supervisor
chancellor	debtor	investor	suppressor
compositor	doctor	manor (house)	surveyor
compressor	donor	mentor	tractor
conjuror	duplicator	meteor	vendor
conqueror	editor	professor	visor (or vizor)

Note: i) [1] *American differences*: carburetor for carburettor; councilor for councillor; counselor for counsellor; many of British **-our** endings are **-or** to Americans.

ii) Either advisor or adviser is correct, as noted earlier. The same is true with conjuror and conjurer. Abetter may also be used instead of abettor by lawyers.

iii) Councillor means member of a council; counsellor means advisor. Manor means large country house; manner means conduct or way of behaving.

iv) Vender also acceptable, particularly with meaning of vending machine.

d)   -er or -or

A few words take either an **-er** or **-or** ending. The examples of adviser/advisor and conjuror/conjurer have been noted above. There is also conveyer/conveyor.

In other cases, the difference in ending may indicate a difference in meaning. For example:

-er	**-or**
accepter – person who accepts	acceptor – either person who accepts or scientific/technical term
adapter – person who adapts or electrical connection	adaptor – electrical connection
caster – type-casting machine or container for sprinkling contents or swivelled wheel on chair	castor – container for sprinkling contents or swivelled wheel on chair or substance used in medicine
censer – vessel for burning incense	censor – official or magistrate
sailer – ship	sailor – seaman

e) **-re**

Words ending in **-re**, but sometimes sounding confusingly like **-er** endings (in other cases, they end with an [uh] sound), include:

acre	lucre	mitre[1]	sepulchre
calibre[1]	lustre[1]	nitre[1]	sombre[1]
centimetre[1]	manoeuvre[1]	ochre[1]	spectre[1]
centre[1]	massacre	ogre	theatre[1]
fibre[1]	meagre[1]	reconnoitre[1]	titre[1]
goitre[1]	mediocre	sabre[1]	wiseacre
litre[1]	metre[2]	saltpetre[1]	
louvre[3]	millimetre[1]	sceptre[1]	

Note: [1] *American differences*: **-er** instead of **-re** (eg caliber for calibre) in the case of these words. Also, Americans reduce manoeuvre to maneuver.

[2] Metre is the measurement, not to be confused with the measuring device meter in the UK, though meter is used for both in the US.

[3] From the French.

f) **-our**

An ending that usually (but not always) has an **-er** sound but is sometimes confused with **-or** is the **-our** ending. This confusion is perhaps the more likely because UK **-our** endings are frequently **-or** in the US (as indicated below).

Examples of **-our** endings are:

behaviour[1]	flavour[1]	labour[1]	rigour[1]
candour[1]	glamour[1]	neighbour[1]	savour[1]
clamour[1]	honour[1]	our	succour[1]
colour[1]	hour	pompadour	valour[1]
demeanour[1]	humour[1]	rancour[1]	vigour[1]

[1]*American difference*: **-or** for **-our** (eg behavior for behaviour).

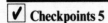 **Checkpoints 5**

In 1 to 5 below, two words only in each group of four are correct.
Which are correct and which incorrect?

1. (a) peculier   (b) celler
    (c) sonar   (d) proper

2. (a) grammer   (b) barter
    (c) launcher   (d) crediter

3. (a) meager   (b) acre
    (c) theater   (d) incubator

4. (a) debter   (b) saber
    (c) gaoler   (d) calendar

5. (a) author   (b) writor
    (c) flavour   (d) buyar

In 6 to 10, which of the words *in italics* are correctly spelt and which
incorrectly? Correct the latter.

6. *Jocular* and *familier* he may have been, but the *vicor* did sometimes
behave in the manner of a *tsar*.

7. The *banker* and the *invester* provide the *lucer*, the *farmer* the
tracters, the *docter* the diagnosis, and the *surveyer* the calculation of
metres.

8. *Compositers* and *printers* do not deign to use *duplicators* for *color*
printing.

9. *Flyers* and *drivors* operate at different levels, in a *manner* of
speaking, but each is undeniably *noisier* than a horse *rider*, though
not having to *labor* as much.

10. The *bowler* was grateful that his *fieldars* were hard *workors*,
standing up to the *rigour* of their task under the tropical sun with
honor, rather than *mediocer performers*.

In 11 to 15 below, what are the missing letters?

11. (a) lun_r   (b) hott_r
   (c) caterpill_r   (d) prop_r

12. (a) particul_r   (b) bart_r
   (c) conquer_r   (d) vend_r

13. (a) blaz_r   (b) emper_r
   (c) man_r   (d) adapt_r

14. (a) helicopt_r   (b) mete_r
   (c) humo_r   (d) schol_r

15. (a) burgl_r   (b) neighbo_r
   (c) impost_r   (d) propell_r

See page 240 for Checkpoint Checks

6. -ary, -ery, -ory, -ry or -ury endings

Pronunciation is sometimes a good test of the differences between
these spellings. For the most part, though, it is a question of
becoming familiar with the following checklists of common words
with each spelling.

a) -ary

Adjectives or descriptive words ending in **-ary** include:

auxiliary	honorary	plenary	supplementary
contrary	imaginary	primary	temporary
complementary	incendiary	secondary	tertiary
(completing)	literary	solitary	veterinary
complimentary	military	stationary[1]	voluntary
(praising)	monetary	stipendiary	
hereditary	parliamentary	summary[2]	

Note: i)[1] The adjective stationary, meaning remaining still, has to be
distinguished from the noun stationery, meaning writing or
typing paper.

ii)[2] Summary can be either an adjective (eg summary dismissal)
or a noun (and as such listed below). As can military and
stipendiary.

iii) Note the two different but often confused words
complementary (completing or balancing) and complimentary
(praising or speaking favourably about).

Nouns ending in **-ary** include:

anniversary	dignitary	itinerary	salary
apiary	dispensary	library	sanctuary
aviary	estuary	luminary	secretary
burglary	February	military	stipendiary
dictionary	granary	obituary	summary

b)   -ery

Adjectives ending in **-ery** include:

fiery   rubbery   silvery   summery (of summer)   watery

-ery endings are more common among nouns, including:

archery	confectionery	joinery	refinery
bakery	cookery	machinery	saddlery
battery	finery	mastery	stationery[2]
butchery	fishery	misery	skulduggery
buttery	gallery	monastery	surgery
cattery	greenery	mystery	tannery
celery	grocery	nunnery	tomfoolery
cemetery	hatchery	perfumery	trickery
colliery	jewellery[1]	piggery	

Note: i)[1] Jewellery can also be spelt jewelry (normal in US).

ii)[2] Distinguish between stationery (meaning writing or typing paper) and stationary (remaining still), as noted above.

c)   -ory

Adjectives ending in **-ory** include:

advisory[1]	explanatory	obligatory	satisfactory
auditory	exploratory	olfactory	sensory
compulsory	extrasensory	perfunctory	statutory
conciliatory	inflammatory	promissory	supervisory
cursory	mandatory	respiratory	valedictory

[1]Advisory is the only acceptable spelling in spite of the fact that either adviser or advisor is correct.

Nouns ending in **-ory** include:

allegory	factory	memory	refectory
category	hickory	observatory	repository
consistory	history	oratory	rectory
depository	laboratory	pillory	trajectory
dormitory	lavatory	rectory	valedictory[1]

[1]Valedictory may be either an adjective or a noun.

d) -ry

Adjectives ending in **-ry** include:

dairy   furry   hairy   paltry   wary   wintry

There are also one or two verbs ending in **-ry** (some having a double **r**), such as:

harry   hurry   marry   parry   tarry   worry

Nouns ending in **-ry** include:

chantry	enquiry	hostelry	quarry
chemistry	fairy	inquiry	query
chivalry	forestry	jewelry	rivalry
country	foundry	ministry	sentry
dairy	gallantry	poetry	vestry

Note: i) Dairy can be either an adjective (eg dairy ice cream) or a noun.

     ii) Both jewelry and jewellery are acceptable spellings.

e) -ury

The few words ending in **-ury** are invariably nouns. They include the following. Some are pronounced with a long [u] (eg fury, jury) while in other cases the **-ury** pronunciation is virtually indistinguishable from **-ery** (eg perjury, treasury).

century	jury	penury	treasury
fury[1]	mercury	perjury	usury

[1]Fury is the noun meaning temper, not to be confused with the earlier adjective furry, meaning fur-like.

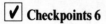 **Checkpoints 6**

Two out of four words in each of 1 to 8 are spelt incorrectly. Which are correct and which incorrect?

1 (a) complimentary   (b) complementery
  (c) celary   (d) tannery

2 (a) summery   (b) honorory
  (c) sentury   (d) rubbery

3 (a) usury   (b) gallantry
  (c) hostelery   (d) vestury

4 (a) auxiliery   (b) finery
  (c) greenry   (d) piggery

5 (a) granory   (b) furry
  (c) harry   (d) valedictary

6 (a) contrary   (b) herediteny
  (c) hatchory   (d) dispensary

7 (a) aviery   (b) apiary
  (c) joinory   (d) advisory

8 (a) ministary   (b) foundery
  (c) query   (d) rivalry

In 9 to 20, what are the missing letters?

9 (a) liter_ry   (b) arch_ry
  (c) annivers_ry   (d) monast_ry

10 (a) cent_ry   (b) us_ry
  (c) mem_ry   (d) prim_ry

11 (a) fish_ry   (b) merc_ry
  (c) butch_ry   (d) hist_ry

12 (a) chival_y   (b) territ_ry
  (c) diction_ry   (d) Febru_ry

13 (a) chemist_y   (b) bak_ry
  (c) fact_ry   (d) pen_ry

14 (a) deposit_ry   (b) treas_ry
   (c) burgl_ry   (d) batt_ry

15 (a) jewell_ry   (b) jewel_ry
   (c) tomfool_ry   (d) fi_ry

16 (a) monet_ry   (b) perj_ry
   (c) forest_y   (d) estu_ry

17 (a) parliament_ry   (b) nunn_ry
   (c) refin_ry   (d) sanctu_ry

18 (a) f_ry   (b) obitu_ry
   (c) chant_y   (d) w_ry

19 (a) vest_y   (b) myst_ry
   (c) wor_y   (d) laborat_ry

20 (a) compuls_ry   (b) stipendi_ry
   (c) secret_ry   (d) summ_ry

See page 241 for Checkpoint Checks

7. -tion, -sion, -ssion, -cian, -tian or -xion endings

Pronunciation is not a very useful test for these endings. They all have much the same [shun] pronunciation. However, there are some general guidelines that can be applied. Broadly, the majority are **-tion** endings with special conditions, described below, applying to the others. One thing all words with these endings have in common is that they are nouns.

a) -tion

Nouns ending with the **-tion** spelling include:

accommodation	imagination	perception	standardisation
accumulation	impersonation	personation	station
administration	induction	personification	stimulation
appropriation	industrialisation	population	stipulation
attention	infatuation	position	sublimation
benefaction	inflection	prescription	suggestion
circumspection	initiation	probation	termination
circumvention	inoculation	procrastination	traction
civilisation	inquisition	promotion	transcription
communication	insemination	pronunciation	transfiguration
competition	legislation	proscription	transformation
conception	limitation	punctuation	transition
condition	locomotion	purification	translation
convection	matriculation	radiation	transplantation
deflection	menstruation	reception	transportation
description	moderation	regeneration	transposition
diction	motion	rejection	tribulation
education	munition(s)	remuneration	vacation
electrification	nation	reorientation	vaccination
expropriation	navigation	restitution	variation
fraction	nomination	resurrection	vegetation
generation	notion	revolution	veneration
genuflection	obstruction	sanction	verification
graduation	occupation	sanitation	vituperation
identification	partition	solution	vocation

b) -sion

A general characteristic of the relatively small number of nouns ending with **-sion** is that they are often formed from verbs ending in **-d**, **-de**, **-se** or **-t**. These nouns include:

collision	derision	pension	subversion
comprehension	infusion	persuasion	suspension
condescension	lesion	profusion	transfusion
corrosion	occasion	pretension	

c) -ssion

Nouns with an **-ssion** ending usually, but not always, come from a verb ending in **-ss** (eg confess, profess) or from one ending with **-t** (eg permit, submit) and derived from the Latin verb *mittere*, to send or let go. Others come from verbs ending in **-de** (eg accede, concede) or **-eed** (eg proceed). Endings in **-ssion** include:

accession	mission	progression	submission
admission	obsession	recession	suppression
commission	passion	regression	transgression
concession	permission	remission	transmission
confession	possession	repercussion	
intercession	procession	secession	
intermission	profession	session	

d) -cian

The few nouns ending in **-cian** and pronounced **shun** are usually used for a person with particular skills or expertise. Such endings include:

beautician	mathematician	patrician[2]	statistician
electrician	musician	paediatrician[1]	technician
Grecian	obstetrician	physician	theoretician
magician	optician	politician	

Note: i)[1] *American difference:* pediatrician for paediatrician.

ii)[2] Patrician is an adjective as well as a noun.

e) -tian

A small number of adjectives have a **-tian** ending. For example:

Dalmatian   Martian

f) -xion

The following nouns have **-xion** endings as alternatives to more common **-tion** endings. Thus:

deflexion (or deflection)   genuflexion (or genuflection)
inflexion (or inflection)

✔ Checkpoints 7

In 1 to 5 below, two out of four words are misspelt. Which are the correct and which the incorrect?

1 (a) personation   (b) suspention
   (c) submition   (d) technician

2 (a) descripsion   (b) vocation
   (c) transfution   (d) permission

3 (a) infatuasion   (b) physician
   (c) possession   (d) remition

4 (a) pension   (b) perception
   (c) resurrecsion   (d) sesion

5 (a) transmition   (b) inducsion
   (c) partition   (d) obsession

In 6 to 10, which are the correct spellings?

6 (a) statian or station?
   (b) occasion or occation?
   (c) transcription or transcripsion?

7 (a) imaginassion or imagination?
   (b) moderacian or moderation?
   (c) accession or accesion?

8 (a) inflexion or inflection?
   (b) dixion or diction?
   (c) probation or probasion?

9 (a) expropriatian or
       expropriation?
   (b) promotion or promossion?
   (c) musician or musicion?

10 (a) population or populatian?
   (b) sublimation or sublimasion?
   (c) initiation or initiasion?

See page 243 for Checkpoint Checks

8. -ous, -eous or -ious endings

All three of these endings usually have an [us] pronunciation, as in bus, this being preceded by an [ee] sound in the case of a few **-eous** and **-ious** endings.

a) -ous

-ous is the ending used (a) with a word or stem ending in a consonant: (b) to replace a silent **e** following a consonant; or (c) after a stem ending in **u** or having **u** inserted before the **-ous**. There are also a few stems that are changed when **ous** is added to them, as detailed on page 142.

Words ending in **-ous** following a consonant, in some cases after a silent **e** has been replaced, include:

ambidextrous	fabulous	meticulous	resinous
analogous	famous	mountainous	ridiculous
androgynous	fortuitous	mucous[1]	scurrilous
anomalous	fungous[1]	murderous	sedulous
anonymous	garrulous	nervous	solicitous
autonomous	grievous	nitrous	sonorous
blasphemous	horrendous	obstreperous	stertorous
callous	indigenous	oviparous	stupendous
cantankerous	infamous	parlous	timorous
conterminous	iniquitous	perilous	treacherous
coterminous	intravenous	platitudinous	tremulous
credulous	jealous	preposterous	venous
dangerous	lecherous	pusillanimous	venturous
diaphonous	luminous	querulous	viviparous
enormous	marvellous	rapturous	vociferous

[1]Fungous and mucous are adjectives. The related nouns are fungus and mucus.

Words in which the **-ous** is immediately preceded by **u** include:

ambiguous	fatuous	mellifluous	sumptuous
conspicuous	impetuous	perspicuous	superfluous
contemptuous	incestuous	promiscuous	tortuous
deciduous	incongruous	sensuous	vacuous
voluptuous			

The two kinds of stem that are changed when **-ous** is added to them are:

i) *words or stems ending in* **f** *change this to* **v**. *Thus:*

grief − grievous   mischief − mischievous

ii) *words or stems ending in* **-our** *drop this* **u** *when adding* **-ous**. *Thus:*

clamour¹ − clamorous	rancour¹ − rancorous
glamour¹ − glamorous	rigour¹ − rigorous
humour¹ − humorous	vigour¹ − vigorous

¹*American differences*: no **u** in the stem in the first place (eg clamor, glamor, humor, rancor, rigor, vigor).

b)   -eous

Easiest to distinguish from the **-ous** endings are the **-eous** endings in which the **e** is clearly pronounced **ee**. These include:

aqueous	cutaneous	nauseous	simultaneous
beauteous	erroneous	piteous	spontaneous
bounteous	hideous	plenteous	vitreous
courteous	miscellaneous	righteous	

Or the **e** in **-eous** may be a silent **e** retained to keep the preceding **g** soft, as in:

advantageous   courageous   gorgeous   outrageous

c) -ious

A few **-ious** endings occur because words or stems ending in **y** change this letter to **i** when **-ous** is added. The resulting **-ious** endings include:

calumny – calumnious	obsequy – obsequious
envy – envious	perfidy – perfidious
fury – furious	study – studious
harmony – harmonious	vary – various
mystery – mysterious	

As with some of the earlier **-eous** endings, in the above **-ious** endings the **i** is pronounced **ee**. However, remembering the **i** for **y** rule in the above **-ious** will help to avoid confusion with **-eous**.

Less helpful is the fact that there are also some other **- ious** endings in which the **i** is pronounced deceptively like the **e** in **-eous**. The following is a checklist of the most common of these particular **-ious** endings.

bilious	illustrious	omnifarious	serious
ceremonious	impecunious	opprobrious	spurious
commodious	imperious	penurious	supercilious
curious	impervious	previous	vicarious
delirious	invidious	rumbustious	
fastidious	lascivious	salubrious	
hilarious	notorious	sanctimonious	

There are also one or two special cases where the **i** is pronounced, but long as in **bite**:

pious

CHAPTER 12

Another group of words with an **-ious** ending have the **i** to keep soft a preceding **c** or **g**. Those with a **c** can be identified clearly as **-ious** endings but those with a **g** may sometimes be confused with **-eous** endings following a soft **g** (page 142). Some of the most common **-ious** endings following a soft **c** or **g** are:

atrocious	irreligious	precocious	tenacious
auspicious	judicious	rapacious	ungracious
contagious	loquacious	religious	vicious
ferocious	pernicious	sacrilegious	voracious
gracious	perspicacious	spacious	
inauspicious	pertinacious	specious	
injudicious	precious	suspicious	

A further group of words take **-ious** but not because they come under any of the above rules (**y** becoming **i**: where the **i** is pronounced but deceptively like an [e] in **-eous**; or to keep a preceding **c** or **g** soft). In this further group the **i** is not itself pronounced (though it sometimes helps convert the sound of a [t] into [sh]), so these are the **-ious** endings most likely to be confused with the **-ous** ending. They include:

adventitious	expeditious	obnoxious	sententious
anxious	facetious	pretentious	subconscious
bumptious	factious	propitious	superstitious
conscientious	fractious	repetitious	surreptitious
conscious	luscious	scrumptious	tendentious

✓ Checkpoints 8

In 1 to 5 below, which of the words *in italics* are correctly spelt and which incorrectly? Correct the latter.

1   Whether *jealous* or *lecherous*, the *senseous* man was *conspicuous* for his *clamorus* and *impetuous* reaction to *voluptuous* women, the more so if *beauteous* and *gorgous*.

2   The *spontanious* response to their *outrageous* and *mischiefous* behaviour was a reaction *impereous*, *ferocious* and *rigorous*.

3   *Courtious* rather than *rancorous*, *garrulus* rather than *obstreperous*, *harmonious* rather than *furyous*, *gracious* rather than *obnoxeous*, *faceteous* rather than *factious*, the protesters avoided a *rumbustious* image.

4   The *enormeous* deficit represented a *dangerous* and *perilus* descent to an *impecuneous*, *unpropitious* and *anxous* state.

5   With *enormus* and *meticulous* care, the team members were *tenaceous* and *conscientious* in their preparation to play before what was going to be a *vociferous* crowd.

See page 244 for Checkpoint Checks

9. -ant

a) Adjectives ending in **-ant** include:

abundant	extant	poignant	resonant
adamant	extravagant	precipitant	resultant[1]
arrogant	exuberant	predominant	reverberant
ascendant[2]	flagrant	pregnant	significant
assonant	flippant	protuberant	stagnant
blatant	gallant[1]	pursuant	superabundant
buoyant	hesitant	rampant	trenchant
cognizant	instant[1]	recalcitrant	vacant
constant	irrelevant	redundant	valiant
dissonant	itinerant[1]	relevant	verdant
distant	mendicant[1]	reliant	vibrant
dominant[1]	militant[1]	reluctant	
elegant	pleasant	repugnant	

Note: [1] Nouns as well as adjectives.
[2] Ascendant can also be spelt ascendent.

Nouns ending in **-ant** include:

adjutant	itinerant[2]	plant	sycophant
attendant	mendicant[2]	propellant[1]	tenant
claimant	militant[2]	protestant	toxicant
currant (fruit)	peasant	refrigerant	transplant[3]
dependant[1]	pedant	restaurant	truant
descendant	penchant	resultant	tyrant
elephant	pendant[1]	ruminant	vagrant
emigrant	pennant	stimulant	variant
fondant	pheasant	supplicant	

Note: [1] Dependant, pendant and propellant are nouns, not to be confused with the adjectives dependent, pendent and propellent (noted later).

[2] As noted earlier, itinerant, mendicant and militant can also be adjectives. So can attendant and, more rarely, refrigerant and ruminant.

[3] Transplant can also be a verb (see below).

There are also a few verbs ending in **-ant**, including:

disenchant	recant	transplant
enchant	supplant	

b) **-ent**

First, **-ment** endings are something of a special case: the **-ent** in their spelling is almost invariably clear from their pronunciation. The spelling problems and rules in adding **-ment** as a suffix have been covered in Chapters 4 and 5 (pages 37 and 49), but there are also other **-ment** endings that are an original part of the word or root, rather than a suffix. They include the following (all nouns except for element, inclement and vehement):

cement	foment	predicament	temperament
clement	garment	presentiment	tenement
comment	inclement	raiment	torment
detriment	lament	sediment	tournament
element	monument	supplement	vehement

Each of the above is normally pronounced with a clear **- ent** ending. On the other hand, the few words with a **mant** ending (eg adamant, claimant) tend to have the more blurred **- unt** pronunciation.

Other **-ent** endings are not always crystal clear from their pronunciation.

Adjectives with **-ent** endings include:

absent	emergent	nascent	recurrent
abstinent	eminent	obedient	redolent
apparent	equivalent[1]	omnipotent	reminiscent
ardent	evident	omnipresent	renascent
belligerent	excellent	omniscient	repellent
beneficent	expedient	patient[1]	resilient
benevolent	flatulent	pendent[2]	resplendent
coherent	fluorescent	penitent	resurgent
competent	frequent	percipient	reticent
consequent	imminent	permanent	reverent
consistent	impotent	pertinent	salient[1]
content[1]	impudent	phosphorescent	sapient
current[3]	inadvertent	pre-eminent	sentient
decadent	incandescent	prescient	strident
decent	incipient[4]	present	stringent
deficient	independent	proficient	subsequent
delinquent[1]	indigent	propellent[2]	subservient
dependent[2]	inefficient	provident	succulent
deterrent[1]	insipient[4]	prudent	transient
different	insolent	prurient	transparent
diffident	latent	pungent	truculent
diligent	lenient	putrescent	turbulent
dissident[1]	magnificent	quiescent	urgent
efficient	munificent	recent	

Note: [1] These particular words can be nouns as well as adjectives, though sometimes with different stresses (for example, in the case of content; the adjective, meaning happy, has the stress on the second syllable; the noun, meaning what is included, stresses on the first).

[2] The adjectives dependent, pendent and propellent have different endings from the related nouns, dependant, pendant and propellant.

[3] Current, the adjective signifying at present, has the same spelling as the noun meaning flow of air, water or electricity. The noun meaning fruit, currant, is different.

[4] Incipient means at the beginning, while insipient means foolish.

Nouns with **-ent** endings include:

ascent	delinquent[1]	orient	regent
coefficient	deterrent[1]	patient[1]	respondent
content[1]	dissent	portent	superintendent
continent	dissident[1]	precedent[3]	tangent
convent	equivalent[1]	president[3]	trident
co-respondent[2]	extent	proponent	undercurrent
correspondent[2]	incumbent[1]	quotient	
current[1]	occident	recipient	

Note: [1] Also adjectives (see above).

     [2] Co-respondent (with a long first [o], as in bone) means co-defendant in divorce suit (*American difference*: corespondent); correspondent (with a short first [o], as in office) means one who writes.

     [3] Precedent, with a soft [c], means preceding in time and/or establishing a practice; president, with a hard [s], means senior official (as in President of the USA or a US corporation).

The few verbs with **-ent** endings include:

cement	invent	prevent	resent
circumvent	lament[3]	relent	
frequent[2]	present[1]	repent	

Note: [1] Also either an adjective or noun.

     [2] Also the spelling for an adjective.

     [3] Also the spelling for a noun.

c)   -ance, -ence or -ense

Distinguishing between **-ance** and **-ence** endings is much the same problem as doing so between **-ant** and **-ent**. Sometimes pronunciation is different, sometimes it fuses into a common **-unce** as in dunce. Often, words ending in **-ance** are related to words ending in **-ant**, and there can be a similar relationship between **-ence** and **-ent** words.

The small number of words with **-ense** endings are pronounced clearly but, of course, may therefore be confused with **-ence**. Indeed, some words ending in **-ense** in British English (as distinct from American) are verbs related to nouns ending in **-ence**.

-ance endings include:

abundance	finance	precipitance	resistance
arrogance	glance	predominance	resonance
askance	grievance	preponderance	romance
appearance	hesitance	protuberance	seance
assonance	instance	pursuance	semblance
attendance	insurance	purveyance	stance
cognizance	irrelevance	reassurance	substance
countenance	maintenance	recalcitrance	sufferance
defiance	obeisance	recognizance	superabundance
dissonance	ordinance	reconnaissance	surveillance
distance	ordnance	reinsurance	temperance
disturbance	outdistance	reliance	trance
dominance	performance	reluctance	valance
elegance	permeance	remembrance	variance
entrance	perseverance	renaissance	
extravagance	pittance	repugnance	
exuberance	prance	resemblance	

Note: Most of the above words ending in **-ance** are nouns.

-ence endings include:

beneficence	expedience	omniscience	reminiscence
commence	experience	opulence	renascence
competence	flatulence	penitence	residence
consequence	imminence	permanence	resilience
consistence[1]	impotence	persistence	resplendence
correspondence	impudence	phosphorescence	resurgence
credence	inadvertence	precedence	reverence
decadence	incipience[2]	pre-eminence	sapience
defence	indolence	preference	sentence
difference	insipience[2]	prescience	sequence
emergence	insolence	presence	subsequence
eminence	licence[3]	pretence	subservience
equivalence	magnificence	providence	subsistence
essence	obedience	prudence	succulence
evidence	occurrence	quiescence	valence
excellence	offence	quintessence	whence
exigence	omnipotence	recurrence	
existence	omnipresence	redolence	

Note: i) [1] The more common alternative to consistence is consistency.

ii) [2] Incipience means beginning while insipience means foolishness (virtually the same point is made above of incipient and insipient).

iii) [3] Licence is the noun; the verb is license, except in the US (*American difference*) where both noun and verb are licence.

iv) *American difference*: some nouns with **-ence** endings have **-ense** endings in the US. For example: defense, license, offense, pretense.

-ense endings common in the UK include:

condense	immense	recompense	tense
dense	intense	sense	
expense	license (verb)	suspense	

d) -ancy or -ency

Again, the pronunciation test is only sometimes helpful in separating **-ancy** from **-ency**. They too often fuse into a clipped (and sometimes grunted!) **-uncy**.

More helpful may be the fact that **-ancy** endings are often from the same family as **-ant** or **-ance** endings. Similarly, words ending in **-ency** may have recognisable links with others ending in **-ent** or **-ence**.

Words ending in **-ancy** include the following (all, incidentally, nouns):

adjutancy	flagrancy	nancy	tenancy
ascendancy	flippancy	piquancy	trenchancy
buoyancy	hesitancy	pliancy	truancy
constancy	infancy	poignancy	vacancy
expectancy	irrelevancy	redundancy	vagrancy
fancy	militancy	stagnancy	verdancy

-ency endings (again, these are all nouns) include:

belligerency	excellency	presidency	tendency
consistency	exigency	proficiency	tangency
currency	expediency	pruriency	transparency
deficiency	frequency	pungency	truculency
delinquency	incumbency	residency	valency
efficiency	leniency	resiliency	
emergency	permanency	stringency	

☑ **Checkpoints 9**

Which letter, **a** or **e**, is missing in each of the words in 1 to 20?

1   (a) claim_nt   (b) itiner_nt
    (c) sali_nt   (d) cont_nt

2   (a) flatul_nt   (b) se_nce
    (c) recomp_nse   (d) leni_ncy

3   (a) eleg_nce   (b) ess_nce
    (c) buoy_ncy   (d) pend_nt

4   (a) insol_nce   (b) appear_nce
    (c) conv_nt   (d) descend_nt

5   (a) arrog_nt   (b) inclem_nt
    (c) effici_ncy   (d) depend_nt

6   (a) insolv_nt   (b) ten_ncy
    (c) curr_ncy   (d) pregn_ncy

7   (a) milit_nt   (b) impud_nce
    (c) incumb_ncy   (d) tend_ncy

8   (a) tenem_nt   (b) arrog_nce
    (c) peas_nt   (d) ramp_nt

9   (a) lam_nt   (b) result_nt
    (c) insur_nce   (d) emerg_nce

10 (a) sembl_nce   (b) vehem_nt
    (c) const_nt   (d) tru_ncy

11 (a) adjut_nt   (b) flipp_ncy
    (c) reg_ncy   (d) consist_ncy

12 (a) expect_ncy   (b) decad_nce
    (c) comm_nce   (d) griev_nce

13 (a) eleg_nt   (b) profici_nt
    (c) domin_nt   (d) restaur_nt

14 (a) insol_nt   (b) belliger_ncy
    (c) ascend_ncy   (d) emerg_nce

15 (a) emin _ nce   (b) mainten _ nce
    (c) succul _ nt   (d) garm _ nt

16 (a) mendic _ nt   (b) transpl _ nt
    (c) monum _ nt   (d) propell _ nt

17 (a) curr _ nt   (b) fin _ nce
    (c) signific _ nt   (d) senti _ nt

18 (a) hesit _ ncy   (b) incumb _ nt
    (c) flatul _ nce   (d) recurr _ nce

19 (a) int _ nse   (b) pregn _ nt
    (c) redund _ ncy   (d) pursu _ nt

20 (a) stagn _ nt   (b) ask _ nce
    (c) prud _ nce   (d) cond _ nse

See page 245 for Checkpoint Checks

10. -ise or -ize; and also -yse

The principal problems with these endings is choosing between **-ise** and **-ize**, and often having a fairly free choice. The important thing is probably to be consistent.

However, there are some useful guidelines associated with pronunciation.

For example, if the [i] is pronounced short, as in kiss, the ending should certainly be **-ise**, as in:

practise (the verb)[1]   premise   promise

[1]*American difference*: in US the verb is practice, not practise (thus, Everton practise but Washington Redskins practice).

The following nouns that have a long [i] (as in bite) or one pronounced [ee] also must take **-ise**:

demise	expertise	merchandise
enterprise	franchise	reprise

This is also the correct ending for such verbs as the following:

advertise	chastise	devise	prise[1]
advise	circumcise	emphasise	televise
apprise	compromise	enfranchise	transistorise
arise	despise	improvise	

Note: [1]*American difference:* to prize (open)

-ise is also correct for the following words, whether used as verbs, adjectives or nouns:

compromise	disguise	exercise	surprise
demise	excise	revise	

-ise or -ize: there is a group of words that traditionally have often been spelt **-ize** in the UK (in some cases, a tradition derived from their Greek origins) but **- ise** is also acceptable and, indeed, becoming much more common nowadays. These words include:

agonise or agonize	fertilise or fertilize
appetise or appetize	legalise or legalize
civilise or civilize	philosophise or philosophize
colonise or colonize	recognise or recognize
criticise or criticize	standardise or standardize

The **-ise** or **-ize** open choice also applies to words derived from the above **-ise** or **-ize** endings. Thus:

appetiser or appetizer
civilisation or civilization
colonisation or colonization
fertiliser or fertilizer
legalisation or legalization
standardisation or standardization

-yse endings are a smaller group; each group with the **y** pronounced like a long [i] (as in bite); each a verb; each, if you want to go into that kind of thing, derived from Greek origins; and each (what really distinguishes it from an **-ise** or **-ize** word) with the **-yse** as part of the stem or root, not a suffix. For example:

analyse   catalyse   paralyse

Note: i) Each of the above verbs form a noun by substituting **-is** for **-e** (analysis, catalysis, paralysis), a change which has the effect of changing pronunciation of the **y** to a short [i] as in kiss.

ii) *American difference*: **-yze** instead of **- yse**: thus, analyze, catalyze, paralyze.

✔ Checkpoints 10

What are the missing letters below?

1 (a) adverti_e   (b) circumci_e
   (c) transistori_e   (d) catal_se

2 (a) standardi_e   (b) demi_e
   (c) repri_e   (d) legali_e

3 (a) civili_ation   (b) anal_sis
   (c) fertili_er   (d) advi_e

4 (a) chasti_e   (b) disgui_e
   (c) surpri_e   (d) improvi_e

5 (a) revi_e   (b) legali_e
   (c) enterpri_e   (d) appeti_er

See page 246 for Checkpoint Checks

11. -y, -ey, -ie or -ee endings

Endings with an [-ee] pronunciation may have any of the spellings
-y, **-ey**, **-ie** or **-ee**.

a) -y

Examples of **-y** endings are the **-ly** endings in Chapter 3 (page 23);
the **-ary**, **-ery**, **-ory**, **-ry** and **-ury** endings earlier in this chapter
(page 132); and the **-efy** and **-ify** endings next in this chapter.

In Chapter 8 (page 67) several nouns ending in **-y** are listed, the
purpose there being to illustrate the difference in forming plurals,
(a) where the **-y** is preceded by a vowel, and (b) where it is preceded
by a consonant (eg (a) alley/alleys or bogey/bogeys, and (b)
ally/allies or bogy/bogies).

Other words ending in **-y** include:

archaeology	idiosyncrasy	revelry
curtsy	merry	runny
ecology	palaeography	trusty[2] (in prison)
ecstasy	peony	whisky (in Scotland)
fogy	privy	
horsy[1]	prophecy (the noun)	

Note: i)[1] Horsy can also be spelt horsey.

ii)[2] Trusty, as in prison, is not to be confused with trustee, one
who holds a property in trust for another.

iii) Prophecy, the noun, should not be confused with prophesy,
the verb, in which the **y** is pronounced like a long [i], as in bite.

y endings, but pronounced like a long [i], as in sigh, include:

cry   prophesy (the verb)   pry   sky   spry

b) -ey

Examples of **-ey** include:

Anglesey	jockey	money	whiskey (in Ireland
bogey	key	palfrey	and the US)
parley			

There are also a few **-ey** endings with an [ay] pronunciation, such as:

fey	grey[1]	osprey	prey (as in bird of)

[1] *American difference:* gray for grey

c) -ie

Examples of **-ie** endings pronounced [ee] include:

bogie[1] (train wheels)   laddie   lassie   zombie

[1] Not to be confused with bogy (ghostly form) or bogey (golf).

-ie is also sometimes pronounced like a long [i], as in:

lie	pie	tie

d) -ee

Examples of **-ee** endings and pronunciations include:

agree	detainee	free	Pharisee
apogee	employee	interviewee	referee
appointee	evacuee	licensee	repartee
decree	filigree	nominee	spree
degree	flee	Parsee	trustee

Note: An [-ee] pronunciation not spelt that way is quay.

Checkpoints 11

Are the words *in italics* in 1 to 5 correct?

1 The *lady jockies* were *happey* to give a *curtsy* in spite of their *horsey* clothes and their restless *palfreys*.

2 A *gray privy* is probably a *sorry* sight for lovers of either *ecologie* or *archaeology*.

3 The *lackie* had the *key* to both the *whisky* and the *whiskey* cupboards but not the money to buy any.

4 *Idiosyncrasy* gave way to *ecstasie* as the *prophesy* was realised.

5 The *licensey* saw himself as a *referee* between revellers on a drinking *sprey* and a *trusty* of the well- being of his employees.

See page 247 for Checkpoint Checks

12. -efy or -ify endings

The general rule is **-ify** but the following (with related words) are exceptions:

a) -efy

liquefy	– liquefied	liquefying	liquefaction	liquefier
putrefy	– putrefied	putrefying	putrefaction	
rarefy	– rarefied	rarefying	rarefaction	
stupefy	– stupefied	stupefying	stupefaction	

b) -ify

Words which follow the general **-ify** rule include:

crucify	– crucified	crucifying	crucifixion	cruciform
dignify	– dignified	dignifying		
exemplify	– exemplified	exemplifying	exemplification	
glorify	– glorified	glorifying	glorification	
horrify	– horrified	horrifying		
modify	– modified	modifying	modification	
nullify	– nullified	nullifying	nullification	
pacify	– pacified	pacifying	pacification	pacificatory
petrify	– petrified	petrifying	petrification	
rectify	– rectified	rectifying	rectification	
solidify	– solidified	solidifying	solidification	
terrify	– terrified	terrifying	terrifically	

Checkpoints 12

What are the missing letters, **e** or **i**, in the following?

1 (a) pac_fying   (b) dign_fy
   (c) rar_fying   (d) putr_fy

2 (a) glor_fication   (b) stup_fied
   (c) mod_fication   (d) liqu_fy

3 (a) null_fy   (b) solid_fied
   (c) glor_fying   (d) petr_fy

4 (a) horr_fy   (b) terr_fied
   (c) cruc_form   (d) stup_fy

5 (a) rar_fy   (b) cruc_fy
   (c) terr_fy   (d) exempl_fy

See page 247 for Checkpoint Checks

13. -ed or -t endings

-ed is the form more often used to form the past tense or the past participle of a verb. Thus:

back − backed	happen − happened
demand − demanded	kick − kicked
enjoy − enjoyed	offend − offended

Or **-ed** may be used to form an adjective from a noun or verb (sometimes the **-ed** serves either purpose, forming either a past tense or an adjective). Thus:

age − aged[1]	dent − dented	name − named
cripple − crippled	learn − learned[1]	scent − scented

[1]In the case of aged and learned, the past tense and the adjective have distinctly different pronunciations, the adjective (eg aged parent, learned teacher) has a clear **-ed** sound (as in bed) for a final syllable.

However, there are some verbs that may form the past tense with a **-t** ending, instead of **-ed**, or offer a choice between the two endings. They include:

burn − burnt	lean − leant	smell − smelt
deal − dealt[1]	leap − leapt	spell − spelt
dream − dreamt	learn − learnt	spend − spent[1]
dwell − dwelt[1]	lend − lent[1]	spill − spilt
kneel − knelt[2]	send − sent[1]	spoil − spoilt

Note: i) The **-t** ending is the only correct one for the above words marked with an [1].

ii) Kneel[2] can take either ending in British English but (*American difference*) only the **-ed** ending in American English.

iii) The other verbs in the above list can take either the **-t** shown or **-ed**, the best guide being to spell how you pronounce. Or, to play safe, use **-ed** except for the words marked above (ie dwelt, knelt, lent, spent).

✔ Checkpoints 13

Complete the words *in italics* in 1 to 5 by adding either **-ed** or **-t**.

1 They *leap_* into action when the alarm *sound_* and they *smel_* danger.

2 *Crippl___* by fatigue, the *ag___* footballers no longer *jump___* about or *dream___* of success, and gladly *settl___* for a draw.

3 *Present___* with the highest honour in the land, the *learn___* scholars *knel_* in a respect *render___* sweet by their success.

4 *Spil_* engine oil and *dent___* and *burn_* out cars *len_* testimony to what *happen___* when drivers *command___* too much power.

5 *Spoil_* ballot papers *figur___* prominently in the election analysis *demand___* by *frustrat___* electors.

   See page 248 for Checkpoint Checks

13. When to use an apostrophe

An apostrophe has two possible uses:

    1. to indicate that a letter or letters have been left out, that the text has been thus abbreviated or contracted; or

    2. in the possessive or genitive case to indicate possession or ownership of something. These uses are considered below.

1. To indicate that a letter or letters have been left out

For example, in the question 'What's an apostrophe for?' the apostrophe indicates that 'What's' is short for 'What is' and the **i** has been omitted.

The most common example is: it's = it is

Others include:

can't – cannot	that's – that is	we'll – we shall
don't – do not	they'll – they will	we're – we are
he'll – he will	they're – they are	who's – who is
shan't – shall not	you're – you are	won't – will not

2. To indicate possession or ownership

a) Singular possessors

Thus: an apostrophe's uses = uses of an apostrophe
the man's dog = the dog of the man

The man is the possessor of the dog, and so has an apostrophe **s**.
Use of an apostrophe in this way is normally a matter of adding it
and the **s** to the possessor. Further examples are:

the boy's football = the football of the boy
the manager's microcomputer = the microcomputer of the
manager
the secretary's typewriter = the typewriter of the
secretary
the student's calculator = the calculator of the student

However, possession may be too narrow a concept to describe this
use of an apostrophe. It is also needed in such phrases as:

a week's holiday in an hour's time
tomorrow's match a year's delay

If the possessor already ends in **s**, it is only necessary to add the
apostrophe. For example:

Charles' pen = the pen of Charles
James' football = the football of James

However, it is not incorrect, just more ungainly, to add both an
apostrophe and an **s**, as in:

Charles's pen or James's football

b)   Plural possessors

Something similar happens if the possessor is plural and ending with an **s**. Again, it is only necessary to add an apostrophe after the **s**. Thus:

the students' calculators	=	the calculators of the students
the boys' football	=	the football of the boys
the managers' microcomputers	=	the microcomputers of the managers
the ladies' meeting	=	the meeting of the ladies

But if the plural does not end in **s**, both an apostrophe and an **s** do become necessary, as in:

children's playground	men's room
women's interests	oxen's power

If there are joint possessors of a single object or thing, the apostrophe **s** is added to the second of them. Thus:

Fred and Bill's car   =   the car of Fred and Bill

But if Fred and Bill have separate cars, instead of a shared car, the correct use of the apostrophe becomes:

Fred's and Bill's cars   =   the cars of Fred and Bill

3. Compound or hyphenated words

In the case of a compound or hyphenated word, the apostrophe and the **s** are added to the last part of it. For example:

the major-general's uniform	= the uniform of the major-general
the mother-in-law's attitude	= the attitude of the mother-in-law

(Compare what happens to compound words here with what happens to them when their plurals are formed in Chapter **8.8** on page 79. The plural **s** is not necessarily added to the last part of the word).

4. When not to use an apostrophe

You do not necessarily have to use apostrophes in the names of
major organisations or places. It is acceptable to write:

St Georges Church   or   Devils Island

You don't have to write:

St George's Church or   Devil's Island

But you won't actually be wrong if you do.

Possessive pronouns never take an apostrophe. 'It's' can only
mean 'it is'; this apostrophe can never be used to indicate
possession or the genitive case with 'it'. Thus you cannot write 'it's
weight' when you mean 'the weight of it'; the correct spelling is 'its
weight'.

Similarly, apostrophes should not be used with other pronouns
like his, hers, ours, yours, theirs.

5. The two kinds of apostrophe, (i) and (ii)

To summarise, in:

What's Bill's job?

the first apostrophe − in What's − indicates a missing letter, a
contraction of 'What is';

while the second apostrophe − in Bill's − indicates possession or
ownership (of the job).

☑ Checkpoints

In 1 to 5 below, which words should have apostrophes, and where?

1   Theres no telling the troubles that cant be stirred up if governments
    arent careful and dont follow procedures.

2   The prospects for batsmens high scores werent good while the slow
    and fast bowlers grip on the game wasnt seriously challenged.

3   A few days leave of absence hadnt changed the employees attitude
    to their employers offer.

4   The riders frisky horses ill-fitting shoes didnt give them much
    chance of living up to the trainers hopes for the years events.

5   The companys computer systems potential couldnt be realised
    while the software design didnt perform adequately.

In 6 to 10, which are correct?

6   (a) Jock's sporran *or* Jocks' sporran?
    (b) its time to go *or* it's time to go?
    (c) youre too early *or* your too early *or* you're too early?

7   (a) the secretarie's word processors *or* the secretaries' word
    processors?
    (b) a dog's life *or* a dogs' life?
    (c) they'r'e out of luck *or* they're out of luck?

8   (a) getting it's own back *or* getting its own back?
    (b) who's who *or* whos who *or* whose who?
    (c) children's games *or* childrens' games?

9   (a) St John's Church *or* St Johns Church?
    (b) Jack Jones' house *or* Jack Jones's house?
    (c) his chosen course *or* his' chosen course?

10 (a) What's your? *or* What's your's? *or* What's yours?
    (b) Jack and Jill's tumble *or* Jack's and Jill's tumble *or* Jack and Jills
    tumble?
    (c) womens' rights *or* women's rights?

See page 249 for Checkpoint Checks

14. When to use capital letters

There are clear rules about when to use capital or upper case letters (eg. H) as opposed to small or lower case letters (eg. h). (The terms upper and lower case, incidentally, are derived from the way in which traditional letterpress typesetters have for centuries positioned containers or 'cases' of capital letters above those of small letters in front of them.)

The basic rules on using capitals are:

1. Sentences and Punctuation

a) Use a capital at the beginning of each sentence. For example:

> The whole department worked very hard.
> It is said to be wrong to tell a lie.

Thus a full stop is followed by a capital. So is an exclamation mark (!) or a question mark (?) except where they come at the end of direct speech but before the end of a complete sentence. So, in:

> 'Stick 'em up!' Shouted the gunman

the capital **S** on 'shouted' should be lower case.

But — unless required to do so by one of the other rules below — do not put capitals after a comma, a semi-colon or a colon. Thus it is wrong to write:

> He drove fast, But the car held the road well.

Or: There was nothing to be said; The silence said it all.

There should not be a capital **B** on but after the comma in the first example, or a capital **T** after the semi-colon in the second.

b) Use a capital for the first word in direct speech. Thus:

> The student said, 'Please let me do some more work.'

Or: The policeman asked, 'Do you know this is a one-way street?'

2. Proper Names

a) Use capitals for proper names, eg. of people, places (including countries, towns, cities, roads, etc), proprietary brands, etc. For example:

> Andrew; John Smith; Joan; Dire Straits; London; New York; Britain; Gatwick, Sussex; California; Kellogg's; Persil; Mini; Cavalier; Renault.

As well as the nouns, adjectives of nationality and regional affiliation also normally have capitals. Thus:

> American; English; African; Scottish; Welsh; Mancunian; Kentish; Dutch auction; Turkish delight.

Exceptions are a lower case for 'arabic' numerals and for 'roman' typefaces.

Verbs of national and regional affiliations also normally take capitals, as in:

> Africanise; Anglicise; Americanise; Europeanise.

b) Use capitals for each main word where there are two or more words in the name of a street, place, river, district, mountain, etc. Thus:

> High Street; Oxford Street; Gatwick Airport; River Severn; Grand Union Canal; Vale of Evesham; Birdlip Hill; Brecon Beacon; Sugar Loaf Mountain; Mount Kilimanjaro.

3. Titles

a) Use capitals for titles of people, institutions, etc. Thus:

> Mr Smith; Mrs Jenny Jones; Duke of Gloucester; St Joan;
> London University; Coventry Cathedral; St Johns Church;
> Brighton Polytechnic; Republican Party; Inner London
> Education Authority.

b) Important (but not the subsidiary) words in titles of books,
plays, films, newspapers, etc, should also have capitals.
For example:

> Arms and the Man; Cat on a Hot Tin Roof; The Cost of
> Loving; Dictionary of Education; The Sound of Music; Robin
> Hood and his Merry Men; Gone with the Wind; Daily Mirror;
> Financial Times; The Guardian; Washington Post; News of the
> World; Never on a Sunday.

Note: i) Where one of the above titles begins with the definite article,
The, as in The Sound of Music or The Guardian, this also takes
a capital.

ii) In many forms of print, it is also common for titles of
publications, etc, to be in italics.

c) Use capitals for titles when you use the titles to refer to a
particular person. For example, you should write
Principal, Chairman, Prime Minister, etc, if you are
addressing or referring to a particular principal, chairman
or prime minister. If you are referring to such people in
general, do not use capitals.

4. Days, Months, Seasons

Use capitals for days of the week and months. For example:

> Tuesday; Wednesday; Friday; February; April; December.

Do not use capitals for seasons. You should write:

> spring; summer; autumn; winter.

5. Geography and Compass Points

Use capitals for regions described by geographical location. Thus:

Jobs are scarce in the North East (or North-East) and in West Wales.

Geographical locations composed of two or more compass points can be hyphenated in spite of the capitals: eg, North-East, South-West. When used as compass directions only the same terms would not have capitals: eg, north-east, south-west.

✓ Checkpoints

Where are capitals needed or used wrongly in 1 to 10 below?

1 It was raining hard in Trafalgar square. The students from various Universities and Polytechnics were getting very wet.

2 The consequences were clear: Mounting inflation hitting everyone; High unemployment in depressed areas; And inadequate public services! it was a frightening prospect.

3 What could the Batsmen do against such fiery bowling? wear armour, perhaps?

4 'do you want all the road?' Called the furious ferrari driver, Adam smith, hurrying to get to Heathrow airport.

5 eight men in a small boat on the river thames were glad it was high Summer with henley round the next bend.

6 Mr harry brown replied, 'we're already half way down Regent street, with piccadilly almost in sight.'

7 The americanised Cornishman declared, 'Mr Chairman, you are one of the worst Chairmen I have ever met!'

8 Reading the daily telegraph in Westminster cathedral is frowned upon by Bishops and Canons alike.

9 Mondays and wednesdays were early closing days except in august and the Winter months.

10 The Arabian dhow was a surprising sight heading South East for the Indian ocean down the rivers of east Africa.

See page 250 for Checkpoint Checks

15. When to use hyphens

There are three distinct types of situation where a decision is required on whether to use a hyphen:

1. When using certain prefixes
2. When adding certain suffixes
3. When uniting words in compound forms.

In the case of (iii) in particular, as part of the general evolutionary process in language development, there is a constant slow shift from separate words to hyphenation, and thence (as also with prefixes and suffixes) to a fused single word. An *American difference* is a tendency to adopt single-word forms faster than in the UK.

Each of the three situations is considered below.

1. Hyphens with prefixes

The prefixes with which the hyphenation question arises more are: **ante-**, **anti-**, **bi-**, **by-**, **co-**, **cross-**, **de-**, **ex-**, **extra-**, **far-**, **in-**, **neo-**, **non-**, **off-**, **on-**, **over-**, **pre-**, **pro-**, **re-**, **self-**, **semi-**, **sub-** and **vice-**. These are covered below, together with the special case of prefixes added to roots that are proper names beginning with a capital letter.

a) **ante-** *(see also Chapter 9, page 85)*

The **ante-** prefix means 'before'. More often than not it is attached directly to the stem or root, but in other cases prefix and stem are linked with a hyphen. The latter include:

ante-bellum   ante-mortem   ante-post   ante-room

Among words that do not require a hyphen are:

antecedent	antedate	antenuptial	anteprandial
antechamber	antediluvian	antependium	
antechapel	antenatal	antepenultimate	

b) **anti-** *(see also Chapter 9, page 86)*

This **anti-** prefix is used to express opposition to the meaning in the root or stem. The general rule here is to use a hyphen only if it is needed to make the meaning clear (sometimes to avoid clumsiness or confusion with a similar word). Hyphenated **anti-** words include:

anti-aircraft	anti-gravity	anti-novel
anti-apartheid	anti-hero	anti-personnel

c) **bi-**

Having the meaning of 'two' or 'twice', the prefix **bi-** does not usually need a hyphen, though it does in the following:

bi-weekly (twice a week), bi-yearly, and is optional in bi-monthly

More commonly, there is not a hyphen. Thus:

biannual	bifocal	binary	biplane
bicycle	bifurcation	bipartisan	
biennial	bilingual	bipartite	

d) **by-**

This prefix conveys or adds the meaning of subordinate, under, minor or incidental. In the following cases there is normally a hyphen:

by-blow	by-form	by-play	by-street
by-effect	by-lane	by-product	
by-election	by-law	by-road	

The following do not require a hyphen:

bygone	byname	bypath	byword
byline	bypass	byway	

e) **co-**

The great majority of words with the **co-** prefix do not separate it from the stem with a hyphen (or it is optional). Three types of occasion when the hyphen is used are:

i) when the root or stem begins with an **o**. Thus:

co-operate[1]   co-operative[1]   co-ordinate[1]
co-operation[1]   co-opt[1]

[1]Spelling without the hyphen (eg cooperate) is also correct.

American difference: the hyphen is incorrect (spelling must be cooperation, coopt, etc).

ii) when the meaning would otherwise be unclear. Thus:

co-belligerent   co-precipitation   co-respondent[1]
co-latitude   co-religionist[2]

[1]co-respondent (participant in divorce case) needs its hyphen to distinguish it fully from correspondent (letter-writer).

[1] and [2] *American difference*: no hyphen.

iii) with the meaning of fellow or shared. Thus:

co-author   co-education[1] co-signatory co-tidal
co-driver   co-pilot   co-star

[1]Coeducation is also becoming a more common spelling.

f) **cross-**

More often than not, the prefix **cross-**, meaning across or against, does call for a hyphen. For example:

cross-bencher	cross-examine	cross-over	cross-talk
cross-breed	cross-eyed	cross-ply	cross-voting
cross-Channel	cross-fertilise	cross-pollinate	cross-wind
cross-check	cross-fire	cross-question	cross-wire
cross-country	cross-grain	cross-reference	
cross-current	cross-legged	cross-section	
cross-cut	cross-linkage	cross-stitch	

There is no hyphen in, for example:

crossbow	crossways	crossword
crossroads	crosswise	

g) **de-**

Having the meaning of undo or remove, the few occasions when the **de-** prefix retains a hyphen are in those few cases where there might otherwise be confusion with a vowel at the beginning of the root. Thus:

de-aerate	de-escalate	de-icer
de-emphasise	de-ice	

More often, however, **de-** drops its hyphen, as in:

deactivate	decolonise	dehydrate	derail
debrief	decompose	delouse	deregister
debug	decompress	demerit	desegregate
decaffeinate	deflate	demilitarise	dethrone
decamp	deforest	demist	devalue
decapitate	defrock	deodorant	devolution
decarbonise	defrost	deplane	
decode	degenerate	depopulate	

h) **ex-**

The **ex-** prefix does not usually have a hyphen except in a few cases where it carries a firm sense of former or exclusion. For example:

ex-captain	ex-convict	ex-sailor	ex-wife
ex-chairman	ex-directory	ex-service	
ex-colleague	ex-minister	ex-serviceman	

Cases − of Latin origin − where the 'ex' is a separate word are:

ex cathedra	ex gratia	ex parte
ex dividend	ex officio	ex voto

i) extra-

Normally taking a hyphen are:

extra-curricular	extra-illustrate	extra-marital	extra-terrestrial
extra-galactic	extra-judicial	extra-sensory	extra-vehicular

j) far-

A hyphen is needed in, for example:

far-fetched	far-off	far-sighted
far-flung	far-out	

k) in- *(see also Chapter 9, page 87)*

The following words, where the **in-** prefix is used to mean within or existing in, normally have hyphens:

in-built	in-group	in-off	in-tray
in-company	in-house	in-patient	
in-depth	in-law	in-swing(er)	

l) neo-

Meaning of a later or revived period, the prefix **neo-** usually takes a hyphen in:

neo-classical	neo-Nazi	neo-Scholasticism
neo-colonial	neo-Hellenism	neo-Victorian

But not, for example, in:

neolithic	neomycin	neotropical	neology

m) non-

The prefix **non-**, giving a meaning the negative or opposite of the following word or stem, is almost invariably followed by a hyphen. For example:

non-acceptance	non-existent	non-resistance
non-aggression	non-ferrous	non-returnable
non-aligned	non-fiction	non-rigid
non-appearance	non-interference	non-skid
non-attendance	non-intervention	non-slip
non-belligerent	non-linear	non-smoker
non-combatant	non-metallic	non-starter
non-commissioned	non-nuclear	non-stick
non-committal	non-observancce	non-stop
non-compliance	non-party	non-union
non-contributory	non-payment	non-usage
non-co-operation	non-person	non-user
non-delivery	non-playing	non-verbal
non-denominational	non-profit-making	non-violence
non-essential	non-proliferation	non-voting
non-event	non-resident	non-white

Exceptions where the prefix links up with the root without a hyphen include:

nonconformist	nonplus	nonsense	nonsuit

There is an increasing tendency for **non-** followed by a consonant to link up into one word.

A few words that normally insert an **e** immediately after the prefix include:

nonesuch   nonetheless

n) off-

The prefix **off-** is followed by a hyphen more often than not. Cases where it does take a hyphen include:

off-beat	off-day	off-line	off-putting
off-centre[1]	off-key	off-load	off-season
off-cut	off-licence	off-peak	off-stage

[1]*American difference*: off-center

But not in:

offdrive   offprint   offset   offshoot   offshore   offside   offspring

o) on-

After the prefix **on-** there is a hyphen in the following words:

on-cost	on-glide	on-line	on-stage
on-drive	on-licence	on-off	on-street

No hyphen is required in the following words:

oncoming	ongoing	onset	onslaught
onfall	onlooker	onshore	
onflow	onrush	onside	

p) over-

Of the large number of words with an **over-** prefix, there are several that take a hyphen but even more that do not. Those that normally have a hyphen include:

over-active	over-exert	over-react
over-age	over-expose	over-refine
over-anxious	over-hasty	over-sensitive
over-cautious	over-indulge	over-sexed
over-compensate	over-laden	over-simplify
over-confidence	over-large	over-solicitous
over-cooked	over-long	over-subscribe
over-eager	over-much	over-valuation
over-emphasise	over-protect	over-value
over-excite	over-protective	over-zealous

The even larger number of words with an **over-** prefix not needing a hyphen include:

overact	overfulfil	overpraise	overstep
overall	overfull	overprint	overstock
overarm	overgraze	overrate	overstrain
overawe	overground	overreach	overstress
overbalance	overgrown	override	overstretch
overburden	overgrowth	overripe	overstrong
overcast	overhand	overrule	overstrung
overcharge	overhang	overrun	oversupply
overcloud	overhaul	oversailing	overtake
overcoat	overhead(s)	oversea(s)	overtax
overcome	overhear	oversee(r)	overthrow
overcrop	overheat	oversell	overtime
overcrowd	overjoyed	oversew	overtire
overdevelop	overkill	overshadow	overtone
overdo	overland	overshoe	overtop
overdose	overlap	overshoot	overtrain
overdraft	overlay	oversight	overturn
overdress	overleaf	oversize(d)	overview
overdrive	overlie	overskirt	overweening
overdue	overload	oversleep	overweight
overeat	overmanned	oversleeve	overwhelm
overestimate	overmantel	overspend	overwind
overfall	overnight	overspill	overwork
overfeed	overpass	overspread	overwound
overfill	overpayment	overstaff	overwrite
overfly	overpitch	overstate	overwrought
overfold	overplay	overstay	
overfond	overpower	oversteer	

q)   pre-

With the prefix **pre-**, meaning before or in advance of, some words take a hyphen but others do not. Those with a hyphen include:

pre-arrange	pre-empt	pre-natal	pre-select
pre-cast	pre-establish	pre-ordain	pre-set
pre-condition	pre-existence	pre-pack	pre-shrink
pre-cook	pre-human	pre-prandial	pre-war
pre-date	pre-ignition	pre-Raphaelite	
pre-elect	pre-marital	pre-record	
pre-eminent	pre-medication	pre-school	

But there is no hyphen in:

preamble	preconceive	prefabricate	preoccupy
precaution	precursor	preform	preprint
precede	predecessor	prehistory	prescribe
precept	predetermine	prejudge	presuppose
preclude	predispose	premeditate	preview

r)   pro-

The relatively rare cases of this prefix, **pro-**, being followed by a hyphen are when the prefix carries the meaning of substitution (in place of) or support. Thus:

pro-cathedral[1]	pro-Conservative	pro-proctor
pro-chancellor	pro-Labour	

[1] Can also be procathedral

More commonly, there is no hyphen, as in:

proclaim	pronoun	proscribe	proverb
proconsul	propel	protract	
prohibit	proscenium	protrude	

s) re-

Most often, the **re-** prefix conveys a meaning of doing again or doing the opposite. The two situations where this prefix takes a hyphen are i) when the stem begins with an **e** (with the danger of the two **e**s appearing to merge in a diphthong if there is no hyphen), or ii) to avoid confusion with another word spelt the same except for the hyphen.

Examples of i), a hyphen between **re-** and **e**, include:

re-echo	re-embark	re-engage	re-export
re-edit	re-emerge	re-enter	
re-elect	re-enact	re-establish	

Examples of ii), where use of a hyphen avoids confusion with a similar word, include:

re-cover	(cover again)	recover (make a recovery or revival)
re-form	(form again)	reform (improve)
re-pair	(pair up again)	repair (mend)
re-sign	(sign again)	resign (leave or give up)

t) self-

This prefix − meaning operating of its or one's own accord, or causing an effect on oneself − invariably has a hyphen. Just some examples are:

self-addressed	self-conscious	self-esteem	self-respect
self-adhesive	self-contained	self-government	self-satisfied
self-catering	self-defence	self-indulgent	self-starter
self-centred	self-educated	self-made	self-sufficient
self-confessed	self-employed	self-possessed	self-taught

u) semi-

Some words beginning with the prefix **semi-** normally take a hyphen while others do not. Those that do include:

semi-basement	semi-detached	semi-trailer
semi-conscious[1]	semi-permanent	

[1]Can also be semiconscious.

Those that form a single word rather than take a hyphen normally include:

semicircle	semiconductor	semiprecious
semicolon	semifinal	semitropical

v) sub-

The few examples of the **sub-** prefix (meaning lower or a subsidiary part of) being followed by a hyphen include:

sub-basement	sub-edit	sub-lieutenant	sub-plot
sub-branch	sub-editor	sub-machine-gun	sub-sequence

There is no hyphen in the following, to take just a few examples:

subalpine	subcommittee	subculture	subtitle
subaqua	subconscious	subheading	subtotal
subatomic	subcontinent	subhuman	subtropical
subclinical	subcontract	substandard	

w) vice-

Uses of the prefix **vice-** with the meaning of a qualified or appointed substitute (eg vice-captain as a substitute for captain) usually call for a hyphen, as in:

vice-admiral	vice-chairman	vice-consul
vice-captain	vice-chancellor	vice-president

but no hyphen is required in: viceregal, viceroy(al)

x) Prefix before a capital letter

A hyphen is usual when a prefix is placed before a proper name beginning with a capital letter. Thus:

anti-European	neo-Nazi	pro-Labour
cross-Channel	neo-Victorian	pro-Liberal
mid-Atlantic	post-Edwardian	
neo-Hellenism	pro-Conservative	

If the prefix is itself part of a proper name, it usually takes a capital but still has the hyphen. Thus:

Anti-Apartheid (Movement)   Trans-Siberian
Pre-Raphaelite

✔ Checkpoints 1

In each of the following groups of four words, two are misspelt. Which are correct and which incorrect?

1. (a) anti-coagulant (b) antihero
   (c) antechapel (d) ante-room
2. (a) bilingual (b) byelection
   (c) antiseptic (d) anti-climax
3. (a) bicycle (b) anti-biotic
   (c) ante-chamber (d) biplane
4. (a) co-operate (b) co-driver
   (c) cobelligerent (d) crossfire
5. (a) cross-roads (b) de-brief
   (c) demist (d) deodorant
6. (a) deicer (b) de-aerate
   (c) crossreference (d) crossbow
7. (a) de-code (b) ex-captain
   (c) ex-convict (d) ex-cept
8. (a) extra-curricular (b) ex-officio
   (c) extramural (d) extra-ordinary

9   (a) far-flung   (b) inbuilt
     (c) in-group   (d) neoclassical

10   (a) noncommittal   (b) non-delivery
     (c) nonresistance   (d) non-smoker

11   (a) nonconformist   (b) nonsuch
     (c) offkey   (d) offshore

12   (a) offpeak   (b) on-looker
     (c) onslaught   (d) on-stage

13   (a) over-age   (b) over-shadow
     (c) prearrange   (d) pre-natal

14   (a) pre-occupy   (b) pro-noun
     (c) re-enact   (d) re-sign

15   (a) self-respect   (b) semi-detached
     (c) sub-committee   (d) Anti-American

See page 251 for Checkpoint Checks

2. Hyphens with suffixes

The suffixes with which the question of hyphenation arises are principally: **-all**, **-away**, **-back**, **-by**, **-down**, **-fold**, **-free**, **-in**, **-less**, **-like**, **-off**, **-on**, **-out**, **-over**, **-up** and **-wise**. Each is considered below.

A slight complication is that in some cases a hyphen is correct to link particular words if the resulting compound word is one particular part of speech (say, a noun) but the words remain separate and unlinked if used as another (say, an adjective). Where there is such a distinction to be made, the part of speech intended is indicated in brackets (*n* for noun, *v* for verb, *adj* for adjective, *adv* for adverb) in the following examples.

Some of the common examples of use of a hyphen are given below for each suffix. Often, however, it is a case of what is most common or fashionable at present rather than what is **'right'** or **'wrong'**.

a) -all

be-all   carry-all (*n*)   catch-all (*adj*)   end-all

b) -away

far-away (*adj*)   soak-away (*n*)
give-away (*adj* or *n*)   take-away (*n* or *adj*)

c) -back

cut-back (*n*)   fall-back (*adj*)   play-back (*n*)   throw-back (*n*)

d) -by

stand-by (*n*)

e) -down

back-down (*n*)	crack-down (*n*)	show-down (*n*)
broken-down (*adj*)	kick-down (*n* or *adj*)	shut-down (*n*)
close-down (*n*)	put-down (*n*)	sit-down (*n* or *adj*)
come-down (*n*)	run-down (*n* or *adj*)	slow-down (*n*)

f) -fold

Use of this suffix with a hyphen, as in ten-fold, is not exactly wrong but it is better to form a single compound word, as in twofold or tenfold.

g) -free

nuclear-free (*adj*)	rent-free (*adj*)	scot-free (*adj*)

h) -in

built-in (*adj*)	phone-in (*n*)	run-in (*n*)	stand-in (*n*)
check-in (*n*)	plug-in (*adj*)	shut-in (*n*)	teach-in (*n*)
drive-in (*adj*)	pull-in (*n*)	sit-in (*n*)	throw-in (*n*)
lead-in (*n*)	read-in (*n*)	sitter-in (*n*)	trade-in (*n*)

i) -less

The hyphen is only retained before **-less** when added to a root or stem already ending with double l. Thus:

shell-less   smell-less

Common examples of the link between stem and suffix being greater, to form a single word without a hyphen, are:

doubtless	guileless	numberless	relentless
goalless	homeless	powerless	tireless

j) -like

As with **-less**, a hyphen is normally only used after double l, as in:

shell-like

More common is a hyphenless single word, as:

swanlike

k) -off

brush-off (*n*)	lay-off (*n*)	rip-off (*n*)	tip-off (*n*)
bully-off (*n*)	lift-off (*n*)	show-off (*n*)	trade-off (*n*)
cut-off (*n*)	pay-off (*n*)	stand-off (*n*)	turn-off (*n*)
far-off (*n*)	play-off (*n*)	take-off (*n*)	well-off (*n*)
kick-off (*n*)	rake-off (*n*)	throw-off (*n*)	write- off (*n*)

l) -on

carry-on (*n*)	hanger-on (*n*)	slip-on (*adj*)
clip-on (*adj*)	head-on (*adj or adv*)	try-on (*n*)
come-on (*n*)	knock-on (*n or adj*)	turn-on (*n*)
drive-on (*adj*)	pull-on (*adj*)	walk-on (*adj*)
follow-on (*n*)	put-on (*n*)	
goings-on (*n*)	roll-on (*adj*)	

m) -out

black-out[1] (*n*)	knock-out[1] (*n or adj*)	shoot-out (*n*)
check-out[1] (*n*)	line-out (*n*)	shut-out (*n*)
cut-out (*n*)	lock-out[1] (*n*)	throw-out (*n*)
diner-out (*n*)	look-out[1] (*n*)	try-out (*n*)
dug-out[1] (*n*)	pull-out (*n or adj*)	wash-out[1] (*n*)
fall-out[1] (*n*)	read-out (*n*)	way-out (*adj or adv*)
far-out (*adj*)	rig-out (*n*)	white-out (*n*)
fold-out[1] (*n*)	shake-out (*n*)	wipe-out (*n*)
hand-out[1] (*n*)	share-out (*n*)	
hide-out[1] (*n*)	shell-out (*n*)	

[1]Can also be spelt as a single word without a hyphen (eg handout)

n) -over

change-over[1] (*n*)	push-over (*n* or *adj*)	take-over (*n*)
flash-over (*adj*)	switch-over (*n*)	walk-over[1] (*n*)

[1]Can also be spelt as a single word without a hyphen (eg changeover).

Similarly, hangover is spelt as a single word.

o) -up

blow-up (*n*)	fry-up (*n*)	put-up (*adj*)
brush-up (*n*)	get-up (*n*)	round-up (*n*)
build-up (*n*)	hang-up (*n*)	run-up (*n*)
built-up (*adj*)	hold-up (*n*)	set-up (*n*)
bust-up (*n*)	hook-up (*n*)	shake-up (*n*)
call-up (*n*)	knock-up (*n*)	slap-up (*adj*)
carve-up (*n*)	line-up (*n*)	slip-up (*n*)
check-up[1] (*n*)	link-up (*n*)	smash-up (*n*)
clean-up (*n*)	lock-up[1] (*n* or *adj*)	snarl-up (*n*)
close-up (*n*)	make-up (*n*)	speed-up (*n*)
cock-up (*n*)	mark-up (*n*)	stand-up (*adj*)
cover-up (*n*)	mix-up (*n*)	summing-up (*n*)
crack-up (*n*)	mock-up (*n* or *adj*)	sun-up (*n*)
dust-up (*n*)	paid-up (*adj*)	tip-up (*adj*)
fill-up (*n*)	paste-up (*n*)	toss-up (*n*)
fit-up (*n*)	pick-up (*n*)	turn-up (*n*)
flare-up (*n*)	pile-up (*n*)	warm-up (*n* or *adj*)
fold-up (*adj*)	pin-up (*n*)	washing-up (*n*)
follow-up (*n*)	pop-up (*adj*)	wind-up (*n*)
foul-up (*n*)	press-up (*n*)	write-up (*n*)
frame-up (*n*)	punch-up (*n*)	
freeze-up (*n*)	push-up (*n*)	

[1]Can also be single words, linked up (eg checkup).

p) -wise

The suffix **-wise** is usually added directly to the root without a hyphen.

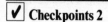 **Checkpoints 2**

In the case of the words *in italics* below, when has a hyphen been correctly included or omitted? And when incorrectly?

1 Will you *take-away* your meal in your *carry-all* or will you *sit-down* and sample the *give-away* prices in this admittedly *broken down* establishment?

2 The *shut down* of the factory followed a *cut-back* in resources, a *sit-down* strike, a reluctance by customers to *stand-by* the company's products, and a management decision to *fall-back* on other production units.

3 The *phone-in* was an opportunity to *play-back* the main points from the *teach in* from *far-off* without getting involved in the *goings-on*.

4 The *home-less* are *powerless* to *slow-down* the widening gap between them and the *well off* and the *hangers-on* of higher society.

5 Straight from the *kickoff* the *stand-off* scored a try that *set-up* a lead from which his side could *head-off* their opponents' hopes of progress in the *knock out* competition.

6 The *share-out* of profits was a *hand out* that led to a *changeover* in the fortunes of the more *worldly-wise* with an ear for *tip-offs*.

7 *Plug-in* and *clip on* devices, some with *fold-up* attachments, were selling fast enough to create a *foul up* at the *checkout*.

8 A *fry-up* may not be quite the *slapup* meal expected by a *diner-out* but it can *speed-up* the *washing up*.

See page 253 for Checkpoint Checks

3. Hyphens with compound words

It was noted at the beginning of this chapter that there is constant, though slow, change in hyphenation, the general shift being from separate words to hyphens and then from hyphenated words to single words (it was also noted that this shift tends to happen faster in American English than British English). This is one reason why it is sometimes difficult to lay down absolutely firm rules and why alternative spelling, with or without hyphens, can be acceptable in some cases.

The best general rule is that a hyphen should be used if and when it is needed to make the sense clear or avoid ambiguity. This is usually a matter of showing that the two hyphenated words are linked more closely with each other than with the other words in the sentence.

Word combinations that usually need hyphenation include the following, grouped according to the parts of speech of the constituent words. If the hyphen only applies when a particular part of speech is being formed by the combination, this is indicated in brackets as earlier in this chapter.

a) noun and noun, usually forming a noun, as in:

alley-way (*n*)	ding-dong (*n*)	north-east (*n*)
argy-bargy (*n*)	drip-proof (*adj*)	notice-board (*n*)
armour-plate (*n, v, adj*)	dust-sheet (*n*)	pack-ice (*n*)
Attorney-General (*n*)	eye-level (*n*)	ping-pong (*n*)
baby-sitter (*n*)	eye-shade (*n*)	pipe-dream (*n*)
baby-walker (*n*)	fashion-plate (*n*)	price-list (*n*)
ball-pen (*n*)	field-day (*n*)	riff-raff (*n*)
bench-mark (*n*)	filter-paper (*n*)	screw-top (*n, adj*)
boiling-point (*n*)	flare-path (*n*)	scrum-half (*n*)
book-end (*n*)	gold-plate (*n, v, adj*)	swing-wing (*adj*)
catch-phrase (*n*)	hanky-panky (*n*)	station-wagon (*n*)
chair-lift (*n*)	juke-box (*n*)	theatre-goer (*n*)
cock-shy (*n, adj*)	knick-knack (*n*)	turbo-prop (*n*)
corner-stone (*n*)	mangel-wurzel (*n*)	U-turn (*n*)
counter-attack (*n, v*)	melting-point (*n*)	whip-saw (*n*)
court-martial (*n, v*)	name-plate (*n*)	willy-nilly (*adv*)

b) nouns and verbs normally linked by a hyphen include:

belly-flop (*n* or *v*)	blood-let (*v*)	joy-ride (*n* or *v*)
bell-push (*n*)	chin-wag (*n* or *v*)	muck-rake (*v*)
cheese-pare (*v*)	house-train (*v*)	

c) noun and participle, sometimes derived from noun-verb combinations in the above examples in (b), can be another hyphenated combination, as in:

blood-letting[1] (*n*)	desk-bound[1] (*adj*)	muck-raking (*n*)
bow-legged (*adj*)	grant-aided (*adj*)	trouser-clipped (*adj*)
cheese-paring[1] (*n*)	joy-riding[1] (*n*)	

[1]Also can be spelt as single words.

Related to some of the above are noun-noun combinations like joy-rider and muck-raker.

d) verb and verb are sometimes hyphenated, usually where the first verb sharpens the meaning of the second. For example:

crash-dive (*v*)	dry-clean (*v*)	hang-glide (*v*)
crash-land (*v*)	force-feed (*v*)	spin-dry (*v*)
drip-dry (*v*)	freeze-dry (*v*)	test-drive (*v*)

e) verb and adverb may be hyphenated, particularly where the resulting word combination forms a noun. Examples of verb-adverb hyphenation include those below, although here too there is a trend towards single words.

break-out (*n*)	clean-up (*n*)	go-slow (*n*)	rake-off (*n*)
bust-up (*n*)	die-away (*a*)	heave-to (*v*)	set-back (*n*)
carve-up (*n*)	dust-up (*n*)	know-how (*n*)	set-up (*n*)
change-over (*n*)	fall-out (*n*)	look-alike (*n*)	take-off (*n*)
check-up (*n*)	fly-past (*n*)	play-off (*n*)	turn-up (*n*)

f) adjective-noun hyphenations include:

all-rounder (*n*)	cut-price (*adj*)	open-air (*adj*)
back-bencher[1] (*n*)	half-back (*n*)	solid-state (*adj*)
common-sense (*adj*)	loose-leaf (*adj*)	

[1]backbencher is also acceptable.

g) adjective and adjective are sometimes hyphenated, as in:

Anglo-French (*adj*)	left-handed (*adj*)	short-sighted (*adj*)
audio-visual[1] (*adj*)	long-sighted (*adj*)	Sino-Soviet (*adj*)
blue-eyed (*adj*)	middle-aged (*adj*)	three-dimensional
cold-blooded (*adj*)	old-fashioned (*adj*)	(*adj*)
deep-rooted (*adj*)	short-handed (*adj*)	two-edged (*adj*)
heavy-handed (*adj*)	short-listed (*adj*)	

[1]Can also be spelt audiovisual.

h) word combinations in which prepositions link nouns, or sometimes verbs, may call for hyphens, as in:

air-to-air (*adj*)	ground-to-air (*adj*)	mother-in-law (*n*)
brother-in-law (*n*)	lady-in-waiting (*n*)	out-of-date (*adj*)
down-to-earth (*adj*)	man-of-war (*n*)	sister-in-law (*n*)
grant-in-aid (*n*)	master-at-arms (*n*)	stick-in-the-mud (*n*)

i) participle and adverb, usually forming an adjective, may be hyphenated, as in:

boxed-in (*adj*)	souped-up (*adj*)
sought-after (*adj*)	tensed-up (*adj*)

j) some pairs of words where the first ends with a vowel and the second begins with one take a hyphen, rather than being linked up in a single word, in order to avoid the possibility of the vowels fusing in a diphthong. Thus:

piezo-electric (*adj*)	radio-element (*n*)	radio-isotope[1] (*n*)

[1]But radioisotope is also acceptable. Similarly, radioactive does not take a hyphen.

k) certain foreign (most often French) compound words take hyphens. For example:

aide(s)-de-camp	fleur-de-lis	post-mortem[1]
aide-mémoire(s)	laissez-faire	sang-froid[1]
après-ski	lèse-majesté	savoir-faire
avant-garde	mal-de-mer	vol-au-vent
bric-à-brac	mange-tout[1]	volte-face
cul-de-sac	passe-partout	wagon-lit
eau-de-Cologne	pied-à-terre	

[1]Can also be single words.

✓ Checkpoints 3

Have hyphens been used correctly in the case of the words *in italics*?

1 A *swing-wing turbo prop* would hardly be the choice of a *stick-in-the-mud* to *take-off* for an hour's *joy-riding* with the *flarepath* extinguished.

2 *Grant aided* organisations have to face up to *cheese-paring* as if they are *short-sighted* enough to *fall-out* with benefactors who are *corner-stones* of their financial backing.

3 The occupants decided to *break-out* into the *open-air* rather than risk being *boxed-in* and threatened with a *dust-up*.

4 People who *hang-glide* usually have the *common-sense* not to *crash-dive* or make a *heavyhanded crash-landing*.

5 *Gold-plate* is more appropriate than *armour-plate* in a *fashionplate*, as the most *short sighted lady-in-waiting* would confirm.

6 A *souped-up man of war* could have a *fieldday* if equipped with *sea-to-air* missiles for *highly-concentrated counter-attack*.

7 If you *check-up* on the *goings-on* among *theatre-goers* they are probably more noted for *sang-froid* than *hankypanky*, short of a dramatic *volte face*.

See page 254 for Checkpoint Checks

16. Acronyms

There is an increasing tendency in some fields to use acronyms — that is, words formed from the initial letters of other words and pronounced as a word, not as the initials. The two fastest growth areas for acronyms are probably (a) the names of national and international bodies, and (b) computer and other new technology terms. Indeed, the names of organisations and new terms often seem contrived to make snappy acronyms. Sometimes the contriving does not quite make it, resulting in a rather forced acronym.

Examples of organisations known more by their acronym than by their name or initial include:

GATT	— General Agreement on Tariffs and Trade
NASA	— National Aeronautic and Space Administration
NATO	— North Atlantic Treaty Organisation
UNCTAD	— United Nations Conference on Trade and Development
UNESCO	— United Nations Educational, Scientific and Cultural Organisation

Though originally spelt all in capitals, as acronyms become better known and more used it may become customary for the first letter only to be a capital. This often happens with, for instance:

Nato, for NATO   Unesco, for UNESCO

Among scientific or new technology terms, some acronyms have passed into such common usage that they are completely lower case or non-capital letters. Thus the word laser began as LASER, an acronym for light amplification by stimulated emission of radiation. And Aids or AIDS is an acronym for acquired immune deficiency syndrome.

Other new technology acronyms and what they are short for include:

ALGOL	–	algorithmic orientated language (computers)
BASIC	–	beginner's all-purpose symbolic instruction code (computer language)
COBOL	–	common business-orientated language (computers)
DIGICOM	–	digital communications system
DOS	–	disc operating system
EAPROM	–	electrically alterable programmable read only memory
EAROM	–	electrically alterable read only memory
EFTPOS	–	electronic funds transfer at point of sale
EMMS	–	electronic mail and message systems
FORTRAN	–	formula translation (computer language)
GIGO	–	garbage in, garbage out (computers)
LAN	–	local area network
LARP	–	local and remote printing (word processing)
ORACLE	–	optical reception of announcements by coded line electronics
PERT	–	programme evaluation and review technique
RAM	–	random access memory
RAPID	–	random access personnel information system
REMSTAR	–	remote electronic microfilm storage, transmission and retrieval
ROM	–	read only memory
SAM	–	serial access memory
VAB	–	voice answer back
VAN	–	value added network
WADS	–	wide area data service
WATS	–	wide area telephone service
WYSIWYG	–	what you see is what you get

17. Homonyms

Homonyms (or homophones) are words that sound alike and may be confused with each other, but often have quite different meanings. This chapter lists the most common homonyms and also includes some pairs or groups of words that, though not strictly homonyms, are the source of similar confusion.

accede	– to take up office (eg the prince acceded to the throne) or to agree (he acceded to the request)
exceed	– to surpass or go beyond a limit (eg his driving exceeded his expectations until he found he had exceeded the speed limit)
advice	– the noun (eg he gives advice)
advise	– the verb (he advises)
affect	– (verb) to have or create an influence or manner (eg he affected an air of disdain, or the sad ending affected them)
effect	– (noun) consequence, impact, property (eg the film had a saddening effect on them) or (verb) to accomplish or bring into being (the actor effected a dramatic entry)
air	– gaseous substance; also derived meanings (eg to air a grievance)
heir	– successor
aisle	– passage between seats in church
isle	– island
allusion	– indirect reference
delusion	– false belief or opinion
illusion	– deception, delusion, misunderstanding of reality

| allowed | – permitted |
| aloud | – with raised voice |

| altar | – table or block used in religious worship |
| alter | – to change |

| analyses | – the plural noun (eg the consultants produced several analyses) or the verb (she analyses the situation) |
| analysis | – the singular noun (they produced an analysis) |

| annex | – the verb or the noun |
| annexe | – can only be the noun |

| bare | – empty or uncovered |
| bear | – strong, furry animal |

| bark | – canine noise, usually with aggressive intent |
| barque | – sailing ship |

| be | – from the verb to be |
| bee | – the buzzing, and sometimes stinging, insect |

| beach | – by the seaside |
| beech | – the tree |

| bean | – the vegetable |
| been | – past participle of the verb to be (eg I have been this way before) |

| beer | – alcoholic drink |
| bier | – wood frame carrying corpse or coffin |

| biannual | – happening twice a year |
| biennial | – happening every second year |

| bite | – (verb) to apply teeth to or (noun) what the teeth have been applied to or the act of applying them (taking a bite) |
| byte | – computer term for group of binary digits |

blue	– the colour or (adjective) down-hearted
blew	– past tense of to blow
board	– (noun) plank, meal table, company directors or (verb) to cover with wood, to provide lodging or to go on board ship
bored	– (verb) past tense of to bore or (adjective) finding something dull and uninspiring (eg he was bored stiff)
bogey	– in golf: also ghostly or devilish figure
bogie	– wheels on the railway
bogy	– ghostly or devilish figure, as bogey
bough	– branch of a tree
bow	– respectful forward inclination; weapon for firing arrows when pronounced 'oh'; front of ship
boy	– young male
buoy	– anchored marker floating in river or sea
brake	– (verb) to slow down or stop or (noun) the means of slowing down or stopping
break	– (noun) fracture or snapping or (verb) to fracture or snap
bread	– staple food
bred	– past participle of to breed (eg Crufts abounds with well-bred dogs)
bridal	– of brides or weddings
bridle	– on horses
by	– preposition or adverb meaning near, alongside, etc (eg by then, they travelled by car, by a wide margin) or an adjective (by-product)
bye	– sometimes interchangeable with by; also (noun) a run in cricket not scored by a batsman
bye-bye	– goodbye
buy	– to purchase

calendar	– record or display of dates through the year
calender	– (noun) pressing machine or (verb) to press
canvas	– the cloth
canvass	– the quest for votes
caught	– act of making a catch or apprehending someone or thing (eg he caught a fish)
court	– scene of legal action, monarch's entourage, enclosed space
cease	– stop
seize	– grab or capture
ceiling	– top of room
sealing	– waterproofing, covering up, etc, or the hunting of seals
censer	– vessel for burning incense
censor	– official for burning books, or supressing them or other written material
censure	– disapproval
cent	– US, etc, small change
scent	– perfume
sent	– from the verb to send
cheap	– low-priced
cheep	– bird sound
check	– to stop; US for cheque
cheque	– bank form
cill	– ledge under window or door
sill	– alternative spelling of 'cill'
cite	– to quote, mention honourably, or summon to court
site	– (noun) ground on which a building, etc, stands or stood (eg the site of the old castle is on the hill) or (verb) to position or be positioned (eg the castle was sited on the hill)

coarse	– crude or unrefined; type of fishing
course	– sequence of events, sports ground, etc
coat	– garment, animal's outer covering, application of paint, term in heraldry (of arms)
cote	– bird or animal shelter
complementary	– making up a whole or balance
complimentary	– giving praise
console	– (noun) cabinet for technical equipment or (verb) to give comfort
consols	– government shares or securities
consul	– representative of country overseas
council	– body of legislators (eg county council) or advisors
counsel	– advice, particularly legal advice, or the act of giving it; person giving advice
crises	– the plural
crisis	– the singular
days	– twenty-four hour periods or periods of daylight
daze	– bewilderment
dear	– expensive; or term of salutation or endearment
deer	– the animal
delusion	– see allusion
dependant	– the noun (eg he has three dependants)
dependent	– the adjective (eg three people are dependent on him)
depositary	– person entrusted with goods
depository	– place where goods are stored
deprecate	– to take a dim view of (eg the government deprecated the attitude of the opposition)
depreciate	– to lose value (eg cars depreciate alarmingly quickly)

desert	– (stress on first syllable) sandy area
dessert	– (stress on last syllable) sweet course
device	– contrivance or design
devise	– (hard 's') to invent or plan
done	– past participle of to do (eg the schoolboy thinks he has done his homework)
dun	– the colour or the horse
drier	– more dry
dryer	– the drying equipment
dyeing	– treating cloth
dying	– expiring, departing this life
effect	– see affect
enquiry	– question
inquiry	– public hearing
ensure	– make certain
insure	– guard against loss, damage or injury
envelop	– the verb, to engulf or smother (eg the defence was able to envelop the opposing forwards)
envelope	– the noun (eg it is usual to post a letter in an envelope)
ewe	– female sheep
yew	– type of tree
you	– second person pronoun (eg you are responsible)
exceed	– see accede
eyes	– means of sight
ice	– frozen water or similar

| faint | – loss of consciousness or being feeble or barely discernible |
| feint | – a diversionary move (eg the boxer feinted with his left then missed completely with his right) |

| fair | – festive or commercial event |
| fare | – charge made for transportation, etc |

| fate | – destiny |
| fete | – festive occasion |

| feat | – notable achievement |
| feet | – what humans and animals walk on |

| file | – documents/information container, metal filing instrument, line of soldiers, etc |
| phial | – small glass container for medicine |

| fir | – type of tree |
| fur | – hairy animal coat |

flew	– past tense of to fly (eg the arrow flew straight and true)
flu	– the illness, influenza
flue	– as in chimney

| flour | – fine powder ground from grain |
| flower | – usually bright and often perfumed part of plant |

| forego | – to precede |
| forgo | – to go without |

| formally | – ceremonially, officially |
| formerly | – earlier |

| fort | – fortified place |
| fought | – past tense of to fight |

| forth | – forward and onward |
| fourth | – after three others |

freeze	— to make frozen
frieze	— decorated edge or strip
fungous	— the adjective
fungus	— the noun
gilt	— gold leaf, secure
guilt	— sense of having done wrong
gorilla	— ferocious ape
guerilla	— (or guerrilla) secret warrior
grisly	— horrible
grizzly	— the bear
hair	— growing from the head
hare	— the animal
hart	— male deer
heart	— organ for pumping blood around the body; also derived meanings such as stout of spirit (eg he is all heart)
heal	— to cure
heel	— rear part of foot
heard	— past participle of to hear (eg I have heard of you)
herd	— number of animals
heir	— see air
higher	— at an upper level
hire	— contract payment for goods or services
hoar	— frosty
whore	— woman of the street
hoard	— store
horde	— multitude

hoarse	– husky, rough-voiced
horse	– the animal saddled by man
hole	– a cavity
whole	– complete entity
idle	– not working
idol	– object of worship
idyll	– attractive scene or relationship
illusion	– see allusion
ingenious	– clever or invention
ingenuous	– innocent, open-minded
jam	– (noun) the food or traffic blockage or (verb) to stop or block
jamb	– door post
key	– for turning in locks
quay	– for landing from ships
knave	– roguish man
nave	– main part of church interior; wheel hub
knows	– present tense of to know
nose	– central feature of face
knight	– male member of nobility (Sir So-and-so So-and-so)
night	– hours of darkness
knot	– in string or rope
not	– negative indication
licence	– the noun in the UK (eg every motorist needs a driving licence)
license	– the verb in the UK (eg licensed to drive) or, in the USA, either the noun or the verb
loose	– not tied down

lose	– to be separated from or no longer have
lumbar	– of the back region
lumber	– timber or elephantine pace
made	– past tense of to make
maid	– young woman
mail	– (noun) the post or (the verb) to post
male	– one of the masculine sex
nave	– see knave
naval	– of the navy
navel	– small hollow in the stomach
night	– see knight
ordinance	– decree or enactment
ordnance	– armaments or related military arrangements
pail	– bucket
pale	– dim or light-coloured
pair	– set of two
pare	– to cut in thin slices
pear	– the fruit
passed	– past tense of to pass (eg the student passed a football more easily than he passed his exams)
past	– what has already happened
peace	– freedom from strife
peas	– small and often elusive vegetables
piece	– part of
peal	– as in bell ringing
peel	– to strip skin, bark, etc
pendant	– the noun (eg she wore a striking pendant)

pendent	— the adjective
persecute	— make life hell for
prosecute	— take to court
personal	— belonging or related to an individual (eg the manager worked it out on his personal computer)
personnel	— body of people or something related to them generally (eg the company needed a big personnel department because it had a large number of personnel)
phial	— see file
place	— position, situation, etc (eg you have a nice place here, or he finished in fourth place)
plaice	— the fish
poor	— having little money or being in an unfortunate condition
pore	— (noun) minute hole in skin or (verb) to study closely
pour	— make liquid flow
price	— the sum paid for goods or services
prise	— to force open (*American difference*: prize)
prize	— (noun) trophy or reward or (verb) to regard something highly or (as with prize) to force open
pride	— high opinion of oneself; gathering of lions
pried	— past tense of to pry (eg the blackmailer pried into the politician's past)
principal	— (noun or adjective) chief (eg the college principal, or the principal objector)
principle	— (noun) basic truth or property (eg the principles of the internal combustion engine have been understood for less than a century)
prodigy	— talented child or talent in general
progeny	— offspring

program	– US spelling for all purposes and UK spelling for computer program only
programme	– UK spelling other than for computer program
propellant	– the noun (eg the rocket needed a powerful propellant)
propellent	– the adjective
prophecy	– the noun (pronunciation ending in 'see')
prophesy	– the verb (pronunciation ending in 'eye')
prosecute	– see persecute
quay	– see key
rain	– as in raindrops
reign	– monarch's rule
rein	– as for controlling or leading a horse
read	– to assimilate written matter
reed	– plant that grows in water or marshes
real	– genuine
reel	– (verb) to wind rope, cotton etc around or (noun) the object around which the rope etc is reeled.
right	– (adjective) correct, (noun) entitlement
rite	– religious ceremony
wright	– craftsman (eg playwright, wheelwright)
write	– to put pen to paper
road	– street, highway
rode	– past tense of to ride (eg he rode through the night)
root	– origin; plant's anchorage
route	– (noun) direction or way taken or recommended; (verb) to send in a particular direction
rough	– tough, clumsy; a person with these attributes
ruff	– frilly collar, or type of bird or fish

sail	— as on a ship
sale	— act of selling
scent	— see cent
sea	— large expanse of salt water
see	— (verb) to have sight of or (noun) area covered by a bishopric or archbishopric
sealing	— see ceiling
seam	— stitched join in cloth or leather
seem	— to appear to be (eg they seem friendly)
sew	— stitch together
so	— to the extent that (eg so far, so good)
sow	— scatter or plant seeds
seize	— see cease
sent	— see cent
sight	— see cite
site	— see cite
sill	— see cill
sole	— alone or the fish or lower part of foot
soul	— of the spirit
some	— particular but unidentified (eg some people may say that); only part (eg there is some sense in that); approximately (eg there were some fifty people there)
sum	— total, arithmetical problem, etc
son	— male offspring
sun	— source of daylight and solar energy

stake	— length of wood or timber; or share (to have a stake in)
steak	— hefty slice of meat
stationary	— standing still
stationery	— writing and typing materials
storey	— level or floor of a building
story	— tale
suite	— set of furniture, a musical composition, or a group of computer programs (suit, pronounced with an 'oo' instead of an 'ee', refers to clothing, the law, playing cards, etc)
sweet	— piece of chocolate, confectionery, etc, or (adjective) sweet-tasting
sward	— expanse of grass (with 'w' pronounced)
sword	— sharp-edged weapon ('w' is silent)
tail	— rear part of animal, sometimes wagging
tale	— story
taught	— past tense or past participle of to teach
taut	— tight
team	— people engaged in united effort; can also apply to animals
teem	— to flow and overflow
tear	— (when pronounced 'teer') as in teardrop
tier	— row or level
tire	— to grow weary; also (noun) US spelling of tyre
tyre	— as on vehicle wheel
their	— possessive pronoun (eg they cleared up their muddles)
there	— in that place (eg he is sitting over there)
they're	— short for they are

threw	– hurled or projected (eg he threw the brick at the window)
through	– penetrated (eg the brick crashed through the window)
thyme	– the herb
time	– as in minute or hour
tingeing	– colouring slightly
tinging	– making a tinkling sound
to	– preposition meaning in the direction of (eg cover-point threw the ball to the wicket-keeper) or an adverb (eg to and fro)
too	– adverb meaning in a higher degree than desirable (eg the bowling was too fast for the batsman's safety) or as well (eg the next batsman scored a century, too)
two	– the number
troop	– gathering of people, particularly soldiers
troupe	– company of actors
trustee	– person responsible for business affairs or property
trusty	– well-behaved and trusted servant, subject or convict
vain	– conceited or without substance or success (eg they protested to the referee in vain)
vane	– as in weathercock or mill, etc, blades
vein	– in which blood flows
waist	– narrower (normally) middle part of human body
waste	– (noun) useless matter, uncultivated land, etc, or (verb) to cause waste or to be wasted
waive	– give up right to something
wave	– hair design, water formation or hand motion
weather	– meteorological conditions

whether	– conjunction expressing choice or doubt between alternatives or outcomes (eg she was undecided whether to go or not)
whine	– shrill sound from animal
wine	– alcoholic drink from grapes
whiskey	– the Irish or the American
whisky	– the Scotch
whole	– see hole
whore	– see hoar
wood	– timber
would	– conditional of will (eg he would, wouldn't he)
wright	– see right
write	– see right
yew	– see ewe
you	– see ewe

Checkpoints

In the following sentences, which of the words *in italics* are correct and which incorrect?

1 One careful *analyses* was enough to tell the *heir* to the throne *weather* he had been well *adviced*.

2 A *coarse* of study at the *site* of the city wall laid *bear* the *root* taken by townspeople in mediaeval times.

3 As the *troupes* marched *forth* they *seemed board* by the prospect of a military exercise that *wood* be a *pail* imitation of the *real* thing.

4   They worked all *knight*, *pouring* over hundreds of documents submitted to the public *inquiry* in order to *check* the *personnel* recollections of witnesses.

5   The *peace* of the evening was shattered by a *peel* of bells and what *seamed* to be *wining* sounds from the kennels.

6   The Minister's resignation had a sensational *affect* on the press when the Prime Minister said he had *exceeded* his powers and policy would remain *unaltared* by what had *bean* an unfortunate incident.

7   The *bored* of directors, though *feint* hearted, made *complimentary* remarks about *their* team of workers to thwart rumours of a *crisis*.

8   Racing cars are *dependent* on good *breaks* to slow them on corners and spare *tires* to *insure* they last the *course*.

9   The *unchequed* runaway *hoarses* disturbed the *heard* of grazing *harts* as it *past threw* them *to* fast for the rider who grabbed in *vain* for the *bridal*.

10 In vain, the fielders tried to stop the progress of the *too* batsmen who swung their bats like *would* clubs at any *loose* bowling.

11 With *brakes jambed* on, the train's *bogey* wheels slid to within inches of the terrified *maid* tied to the rails with a *notted* rope.

12 With the pitch *seaming* to *teem* with opponents, the football *team* realised they were not destined for *hire* things and *wood* have to settle for *forth* place in the league.

13 *Bred* made from good quality *flower* and eaten with *jamb* can make a *cheap* and *holesome* meal.

14 The *isle* in the middle of the *nave* was thronged with people inclining their heads in *boughs* that gave an *illusion* of piety.

15 The city *counsel passed* a vote of *censor* on the *hordes* of *gorilla* fighters who *roamed* the side *rodes* at *night*.

See page 255 for Checkpoint Checks

18. Some unusual or tricky spellings

The basic rules and exceptions of spelling are dealt with in the earlier chapters, and most spellings are to be found there, but the following 100 words are examples of unusual or sometimes tricky spellings.

absence	disappear	koala	pyjamas
accommodation	disappoint	laboratory	questionnaire
accumulate	eighth	lacquer	rarefaction
acquaintance	embarrass	largess	rarefy
aggravate	encyclopaedia	liquefy	recommend
agitator	exaggerate	liquorice	recompense
alleluia	expedient	mackintosh	restaurant
apostrophe	February	marriage	rhyme
archaeology	fillip	medi(a)eval	scallop
aubergine	forbade	mischievous	schedule
auxiliary	foreigner	necessary	schizophrenia
beneficial	gaol (jail)	noticeable	singeing
carcass	guild/gild	novitiate	skiing
chameleon	guillotine	omelette	swingeing
colander	haemorrhage	paediatric	sycamore
comptroller	haemorrhoids	palaeography	taxiing
convenience	harass	paraffin	timpani
conscientious	hearken	parallel	tingeing
consensus	hiccup	peony	transhipment
contiguous	humorous[1]	picnicking	veranda
courgette	idiosyncrasy	pomegranate	vermilion
coxswain	impinging	prejudice	visor/vizor
criticism	inveigle	proletariat	Wednesday
desiccate	jalopy	promissory	weird
dext(e)rous	knowledge	putrefy	wistaria

[1]US spelling: humorus

Checkpoint checks

✓ **Chapter 2** *(page 20)*

1 *receive* and *conceive* are correct; correct spellings of the other two words are *ceiling* and *deceit*.

2 *cashier* and *piece* are correct; the others should be *diesel* and *shield*.

3 *wield* and *conceit* are correct; the others should be *niece* and *priest*.

4 *lieutenant* and *ancient* are correct; the others should be *leisure* and *conscience*.

5 *eight* and *weigh* are correct; the others should be *view* and *reign*.

6 *sovereign* and *skein* are correct; the others should be *forfeiture* and *freight*.

7 *obedient* and *perceive* are correct; the others should be *sleight* and *neither*.

8 *conceived* and *relief* are correct; the other should be *belief*.

9 *receipt* is correct; the others should be *thief* and *conceit*.

10 *freight* and *seized* are correct; the other should be *overweight*.

11 *neighbour's* (US, *neighbor's*) and *deceit* are correct; the first three should be corrected to *sovereign*, *inveighed* and *perceived*.

12 *chief* and *belief* are correct; the others should be *ceiling* and *reviewed*.

13 correct are *gaiety*, *their* and *leisure*; the other should be *friends*.

14 *bier* (the funeral, not public bar, version) and *weird* are correct; the other should be *grief*.

The correct spellings in 15 to 20 are:

15 (a) frieze
   (b) siege
   (c) seize

16 (a) deceive
   (b) receipt
   (c) deceit

17 (a) chief
   (b) grievance
   (c) achieve

18 (a) plebeian
   (b) hygiene
   (c) wield

19 (a) forfeit
   (b) feint
   (c) mischief

20 (a) patient
   (b) height
   (c) leisure

Completing the missing letters in 21 to 25 gives:

21 (a) brief
   (c) besiege
   (b) retrieve
   (d) grievous

22 (a) conceit
   (c) receive
   (b) shield
   (d) tier

23 (a) deceive
   (c) weird
   (b) wield
   (d) protein

24 (a) friend
   (c) view
   (b) proficient
   (d) vein

25 (a) foreign
   (c) eiderdown
   (b) seizure
   (d) sheik

Chapter 3 *(page 30)*

1   *fraternal* is correct but the others should be *eternally*, *grateful* and *expulsion*.

2   *fistful* and *immediately* are correct; the other should be *useful*.

3   *irritably* and *cynically* are correct; the others should be *almost* and *despicably*.

4   *eventually* is correct; the others should be *unfortunately* and *already*.

5   *peaceful* is correct; the others should be *amply* and *wholly*.

6   *cupful* and *readily* are correct; the others should be *hungrily* and *welcomed*.

7   *hopefully* is correct; the others should be *frantically*, *until* and *final*.

8   *dreadfully* is correct; the others should be *colourfully* (US,*colorfully*) and *publicly*.

9   *probably* is correct; the others should be *unhappily* and *truly*.

10 *busily* and *democratically* are correct; the other should be *enthusiastically*.

11 *cancelled* is correct; the others should be *extremely*, *unlikely* and *marvellous*.

12 *jubilantly* is correct; the others should be *chiselled*, *travelled* and *tunnel*.

Correct spellings in 13 to 30 are:

13 a) faithful
    b) faithfully
    c) sackful

14 a) fruitful
    b) bashfully
    c) total

15 a) till
    b) until

22 a) busily
    b) fancifully
    c) basically

23 a) vigorously
    b) coolly
    c) playfully

24 a) flabbily
    b) supply

c) fulfil

16 a) although
   b) playful
   c) wishfully

17 a) gratefully
   b) spoonful
   c) tearfully

18 a) filial
   b) filially
   c) fulsome

19 a) fully
   b) handful
   c) spiteful

20 a) hopefully
   b) generally
   c) skilfully

21 a) definitely
   b) accidentally
   c) heroically

c) bevelled

25 a) channelling
   b) paralleling
   c) signaller

26 a) signalman
   b) signally
   c) rivalry

27 a) skilful
   b) wilfully
   c) shovelful

28 a) carefully
   b) desperately
   c) quarrelsome

29 a) compeller
   b) fulfilment
   c) chilblain

30 a) enrolment
   b) annulment
   c) compulsion

Chapter 4 *(page 39)*

1   *ascribing* and *coming* are correct; the others should be *adoring* and *exciting*.

2   *hoeing* and *tingeing* are correct (if the latter means colouring, not tinkling); the others should be *managing* and *tracing*.

3   *adorable* and *reversible* are correct; the others should be *persuadable* and *removable*.

4   *marriageable* and *serviceable* are correct; the others should be *lovable* and *reconcilable*.

5   *wasteful* and *spiteful* are correct; the others should be *rarely* and *achievement*.

6   *involvement* and *advertisement* are correct; the others should be *excitement* and *argument*.

7   *taxiing* and *scubaed* are correct; the others should be *vetoing* and *mustachioed*.

8   *irreversible* and *timing* are correct; the other should be *rating*.

9   *foreseeing* is correct; the others should be *grieving* and *forgivable*.

10 *singing* (use of voice), *burning* and *singeing* (slow-burning) are all correct.

11 *shoeing* is correct; the others should be *hoeing* and *creating*.

12 *eyeing* and *amusing* are correct; the other should be *discharging*.

13 *noticeable*, *blamable* and *blaming* are all correct.

14 *taxiing*, *scubaing* and *mascaraed* are all correct; the others should be *bikinied* and *skier*.

15 *tiptoed* and *vetoing* are correct; the others should be *videoed*, *commencement*, *duly* and *delicately*.

The correct spellings in 16 to 25 are:

16 a) droning
    b) toeing
    c) framing

17 a) intriguing
    b) judging
    c) grieving

18 a) shining
    b) tingeing[1]
    c) agreeing

19 a) bridging
    b) abridgement or, more
       rarely, abridgment
    c) queueing

20 a) forgivable
    b) hireable (with hirable
       also accepted by some
       dictionaries)
    c) saleable (or, in some
       dictionaries, salable)

21 a) peaceable
    b) peaceful
    c) endorsement

22 a) traceable
    b) tracing
    c) entirely

23 a) judgement (but judgment
       for lawyers)
    b) acknowledgement (or
       more rarely
       acknowledgment)
    c) subtly

24 a) radioed
    b) skiing
    c) echoing

25 a) taxied
    b) appliquéd
    c) echoed

[1]if meaning is to colour slightly but tinging if it is to make a
tinkling sound.

✔ Chapter 5 *(page 51)*

1 *fitter* and *shipper* are correct; the others should be *dropped* and *sipped*.

2 *stewing* and *hitting* are correct; the others should be *arrayed* and *squatter*.

3 *creeping* and *trailer* are correct; the others should be *grouped* and *quitting*.

4 *occurred* and *transferred* are correct; the others should be *committed* and *budgeted*.

5 *picketing* and *targeted* are correct; the others should be *proffered* and *kidnapping*.

6 *granddaughter* and *glamorous* are correct; the others should be *meanness* and *exclamation*.

7 *hoped* and *loping* are correct; the others should be *hopping* and *fastest*.

8 *hooting* and *trying* are correct; the other should be *revved*.

9 *batting* and *falling* are correct; the others should be *slipping* and *staying*.

10 *shining* is correct; the others should be *soared* and *transmitting*.

11 *handicapped* is correct; the others should be *biased* and *budgeting*.

12 *keenness*, *revellers* and *joyously* are correct; the others should be *drunkenness* and *journeyed*.

The correct spellings in 13 to 25 are:

13 a) quizzed
   b) fattest
   c) taxiing is the present
      participle of to taxi, while
      taxing comes from to tax

14 a) arrayed
   b) shopper
   c) tried

15 a) drooping
   b) trying
   c) acquitted

16 a) preferred
   b) preferable
   c) quarrelling

17 a) balloting
   b) bigotry
   c) galloper

18 a) budgeting
   b) marketing
   c) targeted

19 a) regretted
   b) transmitted
   c) beginner

20 a) transferred
   b) regretful
   c) harvester

21 a) focused is correct, but
      focussed is the American
      spelling that has also become
      acceptable in the UK
   b) picketing
   c) worshipper

22 a) committed
   b) commitment
   c) conferment

23 a) glamorous
   b) granddad *or* grandad
   c) vigorous

24 a) annunciate
   b) laborious
   c) entrance

25 a) overrule
   b) stubbornness
   c) kidnapper

✔ **Chapter 6** *(page 57)*

1   *cyanide* is correct; *gypsy* is correct but so is *gipsy*; cristal should be *crystal*.

2   *lynch* is correct; *dike* is correct but so is *dyke*; bycep should be *bicep*.

3   *city* is correct; *tike* is correct but so is *tyke*; cityzen should be *citizen*.

4   *timorous* is correct; *pigmy* is correct but so is *pygmy*; styfle should be *stifle*.

5   *xylophone* is correct; *cypher* is correct but so is *cipher*; lynchpin should be *linchpin*.

6   *joyous* and *enjoyment* are correct; the others should be *journeyed* and *payment*.

7   *prettily* and *paid* are correct; the others should be *busily* and *reliant*.

8   *playable* and *complied* are correct; the others should be *monkeys* and *drier* (but the noun, meaning drying machine, is *dryer*).

9   *slaying* and *dryness* are correct; the others should be *daily* and *slain*.

10 *laid* and *gaiety* are correct; the others should be *spaghetti* and *hungrily*.

11 *unreliable* is correct; *cyder* and *silvan* are correct but so are *cider* and *sylvan*: dryest should be *driest*.

12 *necessarily* and *mini* are correct; the others should be *compliance*, *implied* and *merriment*.

13 *tying*, *drily* and *complying* are all correct.

14 *linchpins* and *cylinder* are correct; plyers should be *pliers*.

15 *unemployed* and *cypher* are correct (but so is *cipher*); the others should be *typist* and *harried*.

In 16 to 18 the correct spellings are:

16 a) trolleys
   b) citadel
   c) bicep

18 a) pitiless
   b) slyly (but slily is less
      commonly used)
   c) dying if the meaning is
      becoming dead, but
      dyeing if it means
      applying coloured matter

17 a) tyre (US tire)
   b) cymbal
   c) paid

In 19 to 25 below, the missing letters are in italics:

19 a) c*y*anide   b) cr*y*pt
   c) c*i*stern   (d) p*i*gmy or p*y*gmy

20 a) s*y*rup   b) Eg*y*pt
   c) d*y*ke or d*i*ke   (d) C*y*clops

21 a) s*i*phon or s*y*phon   b) t*y*rant
   c) c*i*trus   (d) tr*i*dent

22 a) t*i*tter   b) t*y*phoon
   c) enjo*y*able   (d) monke*y*s

23 a) jo*y*ous   b) sla*i*n
   c) lonel*i*ness   (d) merr*i*er

24 a) da*i*ly   b) ga*i*ety
   c) pla*y*er   (d) sla*y*ing

25 a) marr*i*age   b) happ*i*ly
   c) pl*i*able   (d) carr*i*er

✔ **Chapter 7** *(page 63)*

1 *calendar* (record of dates through the year) and *croupier* are correct; the others should be spelt *clench* and *kapok*.

2 *celery* and *kaleidoscope* are correct; the others should be *kowtow* and *census*.

3 *picnicker* and *computer* are correct; the others should be *cod* and *kiosk*.

4 *panicked* and *trafficker* are correct; the others should be *panic* and *trafficking*.

5 *almanac* and *mechanic* are correct (but so is *almanack*); the others should be *cygnet* and *jackal*.

6 *icicle* and *lunatic* are correct; the others should be *yashmak* and *zodiac*.

7 *cricket* and *signature* are correct; the others should be *septet* and *sibilant*.

8 *frolicking* is correct; the others should be *periodically*, *bivouacking* and *soggy*.

9 *connoisseur* and *cut* are correct; the others should be *kebabs* and *snack*.

10 *tricky*, *century* and *shock* are correct; the others should be *wicket*, *quick* and *whack*.

11 *traumatic* and *conduct* are correct; the others should be *erotic* and *cathode*.

12 *karate* is correct; the others should be *dramatically*, *panicky* and *kamikaze*.

13 *kilometres*, *trafficless*, *celebrations*, *trek* and *terrific* are correct; the others should be *racket*, *cymbals* and *city*.

In 14 to 20, the correct spellings are:

14 (a) mimic
   (b) mimicking
   (c) mimicry

15 (a) heroic
   (b) capital
   (c) kaftan but caftan is also
       correct

16 (a) kudos
   (b) cynic
   (c) cyst

17 (a) bracket
   (b) Atlantic
   (c) gimmick

18 (a) politicking
   (b) speckled
   (c) politics

19 (a) curb if the verb, but the
       noun can be either curb
       or kerb
   b) robotics
   c) sarong

20 (a) zinced
   (b) secede
   (c) trek

✔ Chapter 8

1 *(page 66)*

1 *airports* and *files* are correct; the others should be *arrivals* and *entrances*.

2 *balloons* and *wisps* are correct; the others should be *parachutes* and *ghosts*.

3 *circuits*, *fields* and *joggers* are correct; the other should be *antidotes*.

4 *microcomputers*, *printers*, *purchases* and *books* are correct; the others should be *receipts* and *magazines*.

5 *managers* and *spectators* are correct; the others should be *centres* (us *centers*) and *turnstiles*.

8.2 *(page 69)*

1 *galleys* and *underlays* are correct; the others should be *ministries* and *chimneys*.

2 *envoys* and *plays* are correct; the others should be *gantries* and *attorneys*.

3 *boys* and *skies* are correct; the others should be *alloys* and *nineties*.

4 *stories* and *rubies* are correct; the others should be *bodies* and *donkeys*.

5 *families* and *ploys* are correct; the others should be *subways* and *lackeys*.

6 *byways* and *enemies* are correct; the others should be *ponies* and *ladies*.

7 *volleys* is correct; the others should be *valleys* and *monasteries*.

8 *curries*, *rubies* and *eighties* are correct; the others should be *beauties* and *nineties*.

9 *alleys* and *surveys* are correct; the others should be *allies*, *byways* and *enemies*.

10 *trays* and *storeys* are correct; the others should be *trolleys* and *lorries.*

8.3 *(page 71)*

Correct spellings are:

1 (a) varnishes
   (b) buses
   (c) bushes

2 (a) either canvasses or canvases is correct if the meaning is pieces of canvas, but only canvasses will do for the plural of the votes or opinions
   (b) harnesses
   (c) foxes

3 (a) benches
   (b) churches
   (c) premises is correct meaning buildings, but premisses is correct for the bases of statements

4 a) hutches
   b) passes
   c) hiatuses

5 a) crutches
   b) despatches
   c) mackintoshes

8.4 *(page 73)*

Correct spellings are:

1 (a) knives
   (b) either hoofs or hooves
   (c) wolves

2 (a) chiefs
   (b) roofs
   (c) shelves

3 (a) turfs or turves
   (b) wives
   (c) scarfs or scarves

4 (a) thieves
   (b) loaves
   (c) dwarfs or dwarves

5 (a) lives
   (b) selves
   (c) handkerchiefs or handkerchieves

8.5 *(page 75)*

1 *cuckoos* and *audios* are correct; the others should be *cameos* and *stereos*.

2 *curios* and *ratios* are correct; the others should be *videos* and *fiascos*.

3 *dynamos* and *egos* are correct; either *cargoes* or *cargos* acceptable; fourth answer is *mottoes*.

4 *lassos* or *lassoes* and *gringos* are correct; the others should be *scenarios* and *gauchos*.

5 *provisos* and *Eskimos* are correct; the others should be *crescendos* and *oratorios*.

6 *Negroes* and *embargoes* are correct, as are both *zeroes* and *zeros*; the other should be *micros*.

7 *tobaccos* and *radios* are correct; either *mosquitoes* or *mosquitos* acceptable; the other should be *solos*.

8 *impresarios* and *sopranos* are correct; the others should be *dominoes* and *buffaloes* (but *buffalo* can also be both singular and plural).

9 *haloes* and *heroes* are correct but *halos* also acceptable; the others should be *torsos* and *stillettos*.

10 *echoes*, *mementoes* or *mementos*, and *mangoes* or *mangos* are all acceptable; the correct fourth answer is *vetoes*.

8.6 *(page 76)*

1 *men*, *feet*, *women* and *teeth* are all correct.

2 *geese* is correct; but *louce* should be *lice*.

8.7 *(page 77)*

The correct plurals are:

1 (a) fish
   (b) cod
   (c) chips

3 a) salmon
   b) cattle
   c) cows

2 (a) grouse[1]
   (b) sheep
   (c) species

    [1]For the birds, but grouses is the plural if the meaning is grumbles or complaints.

4 In each of the four examples in this sentence, an *are* should be used, not *is*, because these verbs have plural subjects.

5. It is correct to use *is* with economics because economics is one of the plural words normally treated as singular; this is also true of athletics, gymnastics and politics, so *is* should also be used in the rest of this sentence instead of *are*.

8.8 *(page 80)*

1 *mothers-in-law* is correct; the others should be *courts-martial, Major-Generals* and *ding-dongs.*

2 *passers-by* and *men-of-war* are correct; the others should be *lookers-on* and *ladies-in-waiting.*

3 *by-products, by-elections, heart-breaks, change-overs* and *back-benchers* are correct (and, as alternatives to the latter two, so are *changeovers* and *backbenchers*; the others should be *set-backs* and *take-overs.*

4 *micro-computers* (also *microcomputers*), *notice-boards, hand-outs, cross-sections* and *wage-earners* are all correct.

5 *record-players* and *sea-breezes* are correct; the others should be *women-workers* and *look-outs.*

8.9 *(page 83)*

1 *oases* and *plateaux* are correct; the other should be *phenomena*.

2 *viruses* is correct; crisises should be *crises*; *sanatoria* is correct but so is *sanatoriums*; similarly, *mausoleums* is correct but so is *mausolea*.

3 chateaus should be *chateaux*; *cacti* is correct, but so is *cactuses*; *fungi* is correct, but so is *funguses*; *crocuses* is correct, but so is *croci*; and *gladioli* is correct, but so is *gladioluses*.

4 *analyses* is correct; alumnuses should be *alumni*; *hypotheses* is correct; criterions should be *criteria*; curriculums is correct, but so is *curricula*; *syllabi* is correct but so (and more often used) is *syllabuses*.

5 *dilettanti* is correct but *dilettantes* can also be used; *maestros* is correct but *maestri* is also sometimes used correctly; addendums should be *addenda*; corrigendums should be *corrigenda*; *errata* and *bases* are both correct; *formulae* is correct but so is *formulas*; *memoranda* is correct but so is *memorandums*; similarly, *appendices* is correct but so is *appendixes*.

✔ Chapter 9 *(page 96)*

1   *anticyclone* and *antisocial* are correct; the others should be *antecedent* and *anticlimax*.

2   *antenatal* and *antifreeze* are correct; the others should be *antechamber* and *anteroom*.

3   *antediluvian* and *ensnare* are correct; the others should be *anticoagulant* and *encroach*.

4   *enable* and *encircle* are correct; the others should be *enfold* and *entangle*.

5   *initiate* and *engender* are correct; the others should be *involve* and *indictment*.

6   *impair* and *impede* are correct; the others should be *embattled* and *embellish*.

7   *embankment* and *implant* are correct; the others should be *emerge* and *immaculate*.

8   *embassy* and *impulse* are correct; the others should be *immense* and *impetigo*.

9   *unhealthy* and *unrest* are correct; the others should be *unable* and *inability*.

10 *impassive* and *irreverent* are correct; the others should be *immunity* and *illiterate*.

11 *forsake* and *forecourt* are correct; the others should be *forlorn* and *forearm*.

12 *impoverish* and *forcible* are correct; the others should be *impugn* and *foresail*.

13 *anti-aircraft*, *antipersonnel*, *embarking* and *antipodes* are correct; the others should be *antidotes* and *antitank*.

14 *antidepressant*, *antiperspirants* and *antiheroes* are correct; the others should be *anteroom*, *antibiotics* and *antiseptics*.

15 *engine* and *antiknock* are correct; *antefreeze* should be *antifreeze*; *ingender* should be *engender*; *insure* in this sense is correct in the USA but in the UK should be *ensure*.

16 *emitting* is correct; the others should be *enclosed*, *impact* and *embarrassment*.

17 *embedded* and *imperceptible* are correct; the others should be *encrusted* and *unnecessary*.

18 *unreliability*, *unable* and *invective* are correct; the others should be *inability*, *undeniably* and *unjustly*.

19 *embassy* and *forewarned* are correct; the others should be *impartial*, *emissary* and *forearmed*.

20 *forays*, *foretoken* and *forebodings* are correct; the others should be *forecasters* and *forewarnings*.

Correct spellings in 21 to 27 are:

21 (a) antedate
   (b) antipathy
   (c) antepenultimate

22 (a) encourage
   (b) endemic
   (c) ensure in the UK if the
       meaning is to make sure
       or safe but it should be
       insure if the meaning is to
       secure payment in the event
       of loss or damage (in the US
       insure is right for both)

23 (a) indictment
   (b) emaciated
   (c) unflagging

24 (a) implacable
   (b) imperceptible
   (c) improvident

25 (a) illicit
   (b) invocation
   (c) forcible

26 (a) foreword
   (b) forehand
   (c) forehead

27 (a) forefather
   (b) irresponsible
   (c) forerunner

In 28 to 35, the missing letters are *in italics*:

28 (a) ant*e*rior   (b) ant*i*clockwise
    (c) ant*i*cyclone   (d) ant*i*podes

29 (a) *en*slave   (b) *in*trovert
    (c) *im*mortal   (d) *in*coherent

30 (a) *un*rest   (b) *en*counter
    (c) *in*gratiate   (d) *im*minent

31 (a) *ir*regular   (b) *in*tonation
    (c) *im*munity   (d) *e*mergency

32 (a) *in*undate   (b) *in*quest
    (c) *un*limited   (d) *en*case

33 (a) *un*fortunate   (b) *im*personate
    (c) *e*motion   (d) *en*dure

34 (a) i*l*licit   (b) *un*erring
    (c) i*l*literate   (d) *ir*resolute

35 (a) *em*balm   (b) *in*sipid
    (c) *in*nocuous   (d) *un*concerned

✔ **Chapter 10** *(page 102)*

In 1 to 8, the missing letters are *in italics*:

1   (a) *k*nockers   (b) *g*nome
    (c) answ*e*r   (d) *p*neumonia

2   (a) *p*sychoanalysis   (b) *k*nuckle
    (c) *h*eirloom   (d) *g*nash

3   (a) surg*e*on   (b) *k*nee
    (c) *h*ourly   (d) labo*u*r

4   (a) campaig*n*   (b) b*u*oyant
    (c) bisc*u*it   (d) *w*rap

5   (a) *w*rangler   (b) poig*n*ant
    (c) mo*u*lder   (d) play*w*right
        (US molder)

6   (a) *w*reckage   (b) *g*naw
    (c) *p*salm   (d) *h*onest

7   (a) *k*nell   (b) *p*neumatic
    (c) bludg*e*on   (d) *p*terodactyl

8   (a) *k*night   (b) *g*nu
    (c) s*w*ord   (d) *w*rit

✓ Chapter 11 *(page 113)*

In 1 to 15, the missing digraphs are *in italics*:

1. (a) ga*i*ety
   (b) terr*ai*n
   (c) disarr*ay*
   (d) gr*ee*n

2. (a) cr*ay*on
   (b) pl*ay*er
   (c) hoor*ay*
   (d) disob*ey*

3. (a) fr*ai*l
   (b) disemb*ar*k
   (c) h*ear*th
   (d) cl*er*k

4. (a) br*aw*ling
   (b) d*aug*hter
   (c) distr*aug*ht
   (d) rel*ie*f

5. (a) repr*ie*ve
   (b) sh*ou*ld
   (c) ach*ie*ve
   (d) w*ei*rd

6. (a) C*ae*sar
   (b) encyclop*ae*dia (US, encyclopedia)
   (c) arch*ae*ology (US, archeology)
   d) f*oe*tus (US, fetus)

7. (a) law*y*er
   (b) disapp*ear*
   (c) teen*ag*er
   (d) l*ieu*tenant

8. (a) br*ea*thless
   (b) w*ea*lth
   (c) rec*ei*pt
   (d) d*ear*th

9. (a) b*ur*ger
   (b) c*er*tificate
   (c) m*ir*th
   (d) j*our*nalist

10. (a) m*ur*der
    (b) mart*yr*
    (c) handkerch*ie*f
    (d) counterf*ei*t

11. (a) g*ui*llotine
    (b) h*ie*rarchy
    (c) caul*i*flower
    (d) *ei*derdown

12. (a) y*ach*t
    (b) c*oach*
    (c) t*oa*dstool
    (d) sparr*ow*

13. (a) b*ou*lder
    (b) m*ou*lder (US, molder)
    (c) br*ew*ery
    (d) cash*ew*

14. (a) c*ou*pe
    (b) recr*ui*t
    (c) s*oar*
    (d) l*oi*ter

15. (a) pat*ie*nt
    (b) c*ou*rier
    (c) p*ew*ter
    (d) prof*ic*ient

✓ Chapter 12

12.1 *(page 118)*

In 1 to 15 below, the missing letters are *in italics*:

1. (a) avail*a*ble (b) blame*a*ble
   (c) debat*a*ble (d) neglig*i*ble

2. (a) convert*i*ble (b) admiss*i*ble
   (c) insuffer*a*ble (d) adapt*a*ble

3. (a) admir*a*ble (b) express*i*ble
   (c) ed*i*ble (d) comfort*a*ble

4. (a) consider*a*ble (b) fall*i*ble
   (c) respons*i*ble (d) cur*a*ble

5. (a) manoeuvr*a*ble (US, maneuver*a*ble)
   (b) prefer*a*ble
   (c) suit*a*ble (d) suscept*i*ble

6. (a) malle*a*ble (b) perish*a*ble
   (c) destruct*i*ble (d) impass*a*ble'

7. (a) inevit*a*ble (b) inimit*a*ble
   (c) aud*i*ble (d) infall*i*ble

8. (a) despic*a*ble (b) avoid*a*ble
   (c) intang*i*ble (d) percept*i*ble

9. (a) dirig*i*ble (b) divis*i*ble
   (c) reli*a*ble (d) reput*a*ble

10. (a) like*a*ble (b) collaps*i*ble
    (c) vari*a*ble (d) hospit*a*ble

11. (a) appreci*a*bly (b) desir*a*bility
    (c) infall*i*bly (d) reli*a*bly

12. (a) contempt*i*bly (b) like*a*bly
    (c) insuffer*a*bly (d) unmistak*a*bly

13. (a) implac*a*bly (b) notice*a*bly
    (c) indigest*i*bly (d) unshake*a*bly

14 (a) excit*a*bility   (b) compat*i*bility
    (c) irrit*a*bility   (d) practic*a*bility

15 (a) adapt*a*bility   (b) elig*i*bility
    (c) service*a*bility   (d) invinc*i*bility

¹Though note that besides 'impassible', that cannot be passed,
there also exists 'impassible', without emotion, impassive.

12.2 *(page 121)*

1 *advisors* is correct but *advisers* would be too; *practical* is correct; but
adviced should be *advised*, and advise is the noun and should be
advice.

2 *licence*, *practise* (verb) and *endorsement* are correct; but deviced and
licenced (both verbs) should be *devised* and *licensed*.

3 *mongoose* is correct; but practisable should be *practicable* and
ambiense should be *ambience*.

4 *geese*, *liquorice* and *advised* are correct (so, incidentally, would be
licorice).

5 *recompense* is correct; devise (the noun) should be *device*; *licensed* is
correct.

12.3 *(page 123)*

1 proceedurally should be *procedurally* with a single **e**; *succession* is
correct; but conceed should be *concede*.

2 *succeeding* is correct; but excede should be *exceed*, while preceeded
should be *preceded*.

3 *success* and *seceded* are correct; but receeded should be *receded*.

4 *succeeded* is correct; but acceeded should be *acceded* and
proceedure should be *procedure*.

5 superseed should be *supersede*; *concessions* and *intercede* are
correct.

12.4 *(page 125)*

In 1 to 5 below, the correct spellings are:

1. (a) farcical
    (b) icicle
    (c) cubicle

2. (a) clavicle
    (b) barnacle
    (c) miracle

3. (a) vehicle
    (b) comical
    (c) manacle

4. (a) oracle
    (b) article
    (c) mechanical

5. (a) methodical
    (b) obstacle
    (c) critical

12.5 *(page 130)*

1   *sonar* and *proper* are correct; the others should be *peculiar* and *cellar*.

2   *barter* and *launcher* are correct; the others should be *grammar* and *creditor*.

3   *acre* and *incubator* are correct; meager and theater would also be correct in the USA but in the UK they should be *meagre* and *theatre*.

4   *gaoler* and *calendar* (yearly record) are correct; the others should be *debtor* and *sabre* (US, saber).

5   *author* and *flavour* are correct; the others should be *writer* and *buyer*.

6   *jocular* and *tsar* (but also *csar*) are correct; the others should be *familiar*, *vicar* and *manner*.

7   *banker*, *farmer* and *metres* (the units of measurement, not the measuring instruments) are correct; the others should be *investor*, *lucre*, *tractors*, *doctor* and *surveyor*.

8   *printers* and *duplicators* are correct; compositers should be *compositors*; color is correct in the USA but in the UK it should be *colour*.

9 *flyers*, *manner*, *noisier* and *rider* are correct; drivors should be *drivers*; labor is the correct US spelling but should be *labour* in the UK.

10 *bowler*, *rigour* (US, rigor) and *performers* are correct; fieldars should be *fielders*, workors should be *workers*, and mediocer should be *mediocre*; honor is the US spelling that should be *honour* in the UK.

The missing letters in 11 to 15 are:

11. (a) luna*r*   (b) hotte*r*
    (c) caterpilla*r*   (d) prope*r*

12. (a) particula*r*   (b) barte*r*
    (c) conquer*er*   (d) vend*or* (or vend*er* if the meaning is a vending machine)

13. (a) blaze*r*   (b) empero*r*
    (c) man*or*   (d) adapt*or* (electrical connection) or
        (large house)   adapt*er* (person who adapts)

14. (a) helicopte*r*   (b) mete*or*
    (c) humou*r*   (d) schola*r*
        (US, humor)

15. (a) burgla*r*   (b) neighbou*r* (US, neighbor)
    (c) impost*or*   (d) propelle*r*

12.6 *(page 135)*

1 (a) *complimentary* (meaning giving praise) is correct; (b) complementery should be *complementary* (meaning balancing or completing); (c) celary should be *celery*; (d) *tannery* is correct.

2 (a) *summery* is right if the meaning is related to the summer (eg summery weather) but *summary* is correct for the word meaning brief description; (b) honorory should be *honorary*; (c) sentury should be *century*; (d) *rubbery* is correct.

3 (a) *usury* and (b) *gallantry* are correct; (c) hoselery should be *hostelry*; (d) vestury should be *vestry*.

4   (a) auxiliery should be *auxiliary*; (b) *finery* is correct; (c) greenry
    should be *greenery*; (d) *piggery* is correct.

5   (a) granary should be *granary*; (b) *furry* is correct if the meaning is
    having or being like fur (fury means anger); (c) *harry* is correct; (d)
    valedictary should be *valedictory*.

6   (a) *contrary* is correct; (b) hereditary should be *hereditary*; (c)
    hatchory should be *hatchery*; (d) *dispensary* is correct.

7   (a) aviery should be *aviary*; (b) *apiary* is correct; (c) joinory should
    be *joinery*; (d) *advisory* is correct (advisery is not acceptable, in spite
    of the fact that either adviser or advisor is correct for the noun).

8   (a) ministary should be *ministry*; (b) foundery should be *foundry*;
    both (c) *query* and (d) *rivalry* are correct.

The missing letters in 9 to 20 are *in italics*:

9   (a) liter*ary*   (b) arch*ery*
    (c) annivers*ary*   (d) monast*ery*

10 (a) cent*u*ry   (b) us*u*ry
    (c) mem*o*ry   (d) prim*a*ry

11 (a) fish*ery*   (b) merc*u*ry
    (c) butch*ery*   (d) hist*o*ry

12 (a) chival*r*y   (b) territ*o*ry
    (c) diction*a*ry   (d) Febru*a*ry

13 (a) chem*i*stry   (b) bak*ery*
    (c) fact*o*ry   (d) pen*u*ry

14 (a) deposit*o*ry is correct for the more common meaning of a
        storeplace or warehouse, but deposit*a*ry is correct for the
        less common meaning of a person entrusted with goods
                                (b) treas*u*ry
    (c) burgl*a*ry   (d) batt*ery*

15 (a) jewell*ery*   (b) jewel*r*y
    (c) tomfool*ery*   (d) fi*ery*

16 (a) monet*a*ry   (b) perj*u*ry
    (c) for*e*stry   (d) estu*a*ry

17 (a) parliamen*tary*   (b) nun*nery*
   (c) refi*nery*   (d) sanctu*ary*

18 (a) fu*ry* (meaning anger, not to be confused with fur*ry* in 5
    (b) above)   (b) obitu*ary*
   (c) chan*try*   (d) wa*ry* (or it could have been wi*ry*)

19 (a) ves*try*   (b) mys*tery*
   (c) wor*ry*   (d) labora*tory*

20 (a) compuls*ory*   (b) stipendi*ary*
   (c) secre*tary*   (d) summ*ary* (meaning brief description,
                      though there is also summ*ery* meaning
                      summerlike)

12.7 *(page 140)*

1 (a) *personation* and (d) *technician* are correct; (b) suspention should
be *suspension*; (c) submition should be *submission*.

2 (a) descripsion should be *description*; (b) *vocation* is correct; (c)
transfution should be *transfusion*; (d) *permission* is correct.

3 (a) infatuasion should be *infatuation*; (b) *physician* and (c)
possession are both correct; (d) remition should be *remission*.

4 (a) *pension* and (b) *perception* are both correct; (c) resurrecsion
should be *resurrection*; (d) sesion should be *session*.

5 (a) transmition should be *transmission*; (b) inducsion should be
induction; (c) *partition* and (d) *obsession* are both correct.

In 6 to 10 below, the correct spellings are:

6 (a) station
  (b) occasion
  (c) transcription

7 (a) imagination
  (b) moderation
  (c) accession

8 (a) inflexion and inflection are both correct; the latter is more common
  (b) diction
  (c) probation

9 (a) expropriation
  (b) promotion
  (c) musician

10 (a) population
   (b) sublimation
   (c) initiation

12.8 *(page 145)*

1 all correct are *jealous, conspicuous, impetuous, voluptuous* and *beauteous*; lecherus should be *lecherous*; senseous should be *sensuous*; clamorus is alright in the USA but should be *clamorous* in the UK; gorgous should be *gorgeous*.

2 correct are *outrageous, ferocious* and *rigorous*; spontanious should be *spontaneous*; mischiefous should be *mischievous*; and impereous should be *imperious*.

3 correct are *rancorous, obstreperous, harmonious, gracious, factious* and *rumbustious*; courtious should be *courteous*, garrulus should be *garrulous*, furyous should be *furious*, obnoxeous should be *obnoxious*, and faceteous should be *facetious*.

4 correct are *dangerous* and *unpropitious*; enormeous should be *enormous*, perilus should be *perilous*, impecuneous should be *impecunious*, and anxous should be *anxious*.

5 correct are *meticulous, conscientious* and *vociferous*; enormus should be *enormous*, and tenaceous should be *tenacious*.

12.9 *(page 153)*

In 1 to 20 below, the missing letters are *in italics*:

1 (a) claim*a*nt
   (b) itiner*a*nt
   (c) sali*e*nt
   (d) cont*e*nt

2 (a) flatul*e*nt
   (b) se*a*nce
   (c) recomp*e*nse
   (d) leni*e*ncy

3 (a) eleg*a*nce
   (b) ess*e*nce
   (c) buoy*a*ncy
   (d) pend*a*nt if the noun (eg she wore a pendant around her neck) but pend*e*nt if, less commonly, the adjective

4 (a) insol*e*nce
   (b) appear*a*nce
   (c) conv*e*nt
   (d) descend*a*nt

5 (a) arrog*a*nt
   (b) inclem*e*nt
   (c) effici*e*ncy
   (d) depend*a*nt if the noun (eg his children were his dependants) or, less often, depend*e*nt is the adjective (eg he had dependent children)

6 (a) insolv*e*nt
   (b) ten*a*ncy
   (c) curr*e*ncy
   (d) pregn*a*ncy

7 (a) milit*a*nt
   (b) impud*e*nce
   (c) incumb*e*ncy
   (d) tend*e*ncy

8 (a) tenem*e*nt
   (b) arrog*a*nce
   (c) peas*a*nt
   (d) ramp*a*nt

9 (a) lam*e*nt
   (b) result*a*nt
   (c) insur*a*nce
   (d) emerg*e*nce

10 (a) sembl*a*nce
   (b) vehem*e*nt
   (c) const*a*nt
   (d) tru*a*ncy

11 (a) adjut*a*nt
   (b) flipp*a*ncy
   (c) reg*e*ncy
   (d) consist*e*ncy

12 (a) expect*a*ncy
   (b) decad*e*nce
   (c) comm*e*nce
   (d) griev*a*nce

13 (a) elegant   (b) proficient
   (c) dominant   (d) restaurant

14 (a) insolent   (b) belligerency
   (c) ascendancy   (d) emergence

15 (a) eminence   (b) maintenance
   (c) succulent   (d) garment

16 (a) mendicant   (b) transplant
   (c) monument   (d) propellant[1]

17 (a) currant[1]   (b) finance
   (c) significant   (d) sentient

18 (a) hesitancy   (b) incumbent
   (c) flatulence   (d) recurrence

19 (a) intense   (b) pregnant
   (c) redundancy   (d) pursuant

20 (a) stagnant   (b) askance
   (c) prudence   (d) condense

[1] If the noun (eg gunpowder was the propellant) or propellent if the adjective (eg gunpowder was the propellent force)

[2] If the dried fruit, but current if meaning 'now' or 'electrical current'.

12.10 *(page 157)*

The missing letters are:

1 (a) advertise   (b) circumcise
   (c) transistorise   (d) catalyse (US, catalyze)

2 (a) standardise   (b) demise
   or standardize   (c) reprise
   (d) legalise or legalize

3 (a) civilisation   (b) analysis
   or civilization
   (c) fertiliser   (d) advise (or advice if the noun)
   or fertilizer

4   (a) chastise   (b) disguise
    (c) surprise   (d) improvise

5   (a) revise   (b) legalise or legalize
    (c) enterprise   (d) appetiser or appetizer

12.11 *(page 160)*

1   correct are *lady*, *curtsy*, *horsey* (*horsy* is also correct) and *palfreys*; jockies should be *jockeys*, and happey should be *happy*.

2   correct are *privy*, *sorry* and *archaeology* (US, archeology); gray would be correct in the USA, but in the UK it should be *grey*; ecologie should be *ecology*.

3   *key* is correct; so is *whisky* if it is Scotch, and *whiskey* if it is Irish or American; lackie should be *lackey*.

4   *idiosyncrasy* is correct; ecstasie should be *ecstasy*; prophesy rhyming with 'sigh' should in this sentence be *prophecy*, rhyming with 'tree' (that is, the noun instead of the verb).

5   *referee* is correct; licensey should be *licensee*, and sprey should be *spree*; trusy in this context should be *trustee* (a trusty is a trusted prisoner).

12.12 *(page 162)*

In 1 to 5, the missing letters are in *italics*:

1   (a) paci*f*ying   (b) dign*if*y
    (c) rare*f*ying   (d) putr*e*fy

2   (a) glori*f*ication (b) stup*ef*ied
    (c) mod*if*ication   (d) liqu*e*fy

3   (a) null*if*y   (b) solid*if*ied
    (c) glori*f*ying   (d) petr*if*y

4   (a) horri*f*y   (b) terri*f*ied
    (c) cruci*f*orm   (d) stup*e*fy

5   (a) rarefy   (b) crucify
     (c) terrify   (d) exemplify

12.13 *(page 164)*

In 1 to 5 below, the completed words are:

1   *leaped* or *leapt*; *sounded*; *smelled* or *smelt*.

2   *crippled*; *aged*; *jumped*; *dreamed* or *dreamt*; *settled*.

3   *presented*; *learned* (last syllable rhyming with 'bed'); *knelt* (can also be *kneeled*, and has to be in the USA); *rendered*.

4   *spilt* (could also have been *spilled*); *dented*; *burned* or *burnt*; *lent*; *happened*; *commanded*.

5   *spoilt* or *spoiled*; *figured*; *demanded*; *frustrated*.

✓ **Chapter 13** *(page 169)*

1 *There's* no telling the troubles that *can't* be stirred up if governments *aren't* careful and *don't* follow procedures.

2 The prospects for *batsmen's* high scores *weren't* good while the slow and fast *bowlers'* grip on the game *wasn't* seriously challenged.

3 A few *days'* leave of absence *hadn't* changed the *employees'* attitude to their *employer's* offer (or it could be *employers'* if there were more than one of them).

4 The *riders'* frisky *horses'* ill-fitting shoes *didn't* give them much chance of living up to the *trainer's* hopes for the *year's* events.

5 The *company's* computer *system's* potential *couldn't* be realised while the software design *didn't* perform adequately.

In 6 to 10, the correct spellings are:

6 (a) Jock's sporran (assuming there's only one Jock)
   (b) it's time to go
   (c) you're too early

7 (a) the secretaries' word processors
   (b) a dog's life
   (c) they're out of luck

8 (a) getting its own back
   (b) who's who
   (c) children's games

9 (a) both St John's Church and St Johns Church are correct
   (b) both Jack Jones' house and Jack Jones's house are correct
   (c) his chosen course

10 (a) What's yours?
   (b) Jack and Jill's tumble
   (c) women's rights

✓ **Chapter 14** *(page 173)*

1 There should be a capital 's' on Square as part of the proper name, *Trafalgar Square*. No capitals are necessary on universities and polytechnics because they are general terms, not proper names.

2 After a colon and semi-colon, there should not be capitals on 'Mounting', 'High' and 'And'. On the other hand, following an exclamation mark there should be a capital 'I' in *It was* ....

3 There should not be a capital on 'batsman' but, following the first question mark, there should be a capital 'W' on *Wear*.

4 The opening direct speech should begin with a capital 'D' on *Do*, but there should not be a capital 'C' after the quotation marks. As parts of proper names, there should be capitals on *Ferrari*, on *Smith* in *Adam Smith*, and on *Airport* after *Heathrow*.

5 Capitals are required at the beginning of the sentence − 'E' on *Eight* − and on the proper names *River Thames* and *Henley*. There should not be a capital 'S' on 'summer', as a season.

6 Capitals are needed on the proper names *Harry Brown*, *Street* in *Regent Street*, and *Piccadilly*. A capital 'W' is also needed at the beginning of the direct speech.

7 There should be a capital 'A' on *Americanised*, but the capital 'C' is not required on *chairmen* because it is a reference to chairmen in general.

8 Capitals are needed on *Daily Telegraph* and on *Cathedral* in *Westminster Cathedral*. Strictly speaking, the capitals on *bishops* and *canons* are unnecessary because they are a reference to bishops and canons in general.

9 There should be capitals on *Wednesdays* and *August*, in line with the general rule on days of the week and months. The opposite applies to seasons so *winter* should lose its capital.

10 Points of the compass do not normally have capital letters so they are replaced by lower case letters or non-capitals on *South East*. Proper name capitals are needed on *Ocean* in *Indian Ocean* and *East* in *East Africa*.

✓ Chapter 15

15.1 *(page 185)*

1 (a) anti-coagulant is normally *anticoagulant*, forming a single word as is most common with the 'anti-' prefix; antihero is one of the exceptions that normally take a hyphen, becoming *anti-hero*; (c) *antechapel* and (d) *ante-room* are both correct.

2 (a) *bilingual* is correct; (b) byelection usually takes a hyphen, *by-election*; (c) *antiseptic* is correct; (d) anti-climax usually follows the general 'anti-' prefix rule so should be *anticlimax*.

3 (a) *bicycle* is correct; (b) anti-biotic should normally be *antibiotic*, and (c) ante-chamber is usually *antechamber*; (d) *biplane* is correct.

4 (a) *co-operate* is correct but so is *cooperate* without a hyphen; (b) *co-driver* is correct; (c) cobelligerent and (d) crossfire usually take hyphens to become *co-belligerent* and *cross-fire*.

5 (a) *crossroads* does not need a hyphen and neither does (b) *debrief*; (c) *demist* and (d) *deodorant* are both correct.

6 (a) deicer takes a hyphen to become *de-icer*; (b) *de-aerate* is correct; (c) crossreference is normally hyphenated as *cross- reference*; (d) *crossbow* is correct.

7 (a) de-code should be *decode*; (b) *ex-captain* and (c) *ex-convict* are both correct; (d) *except* does not have a hyphen.

8 (a) *extra-curricular* is correct; (b) ex-officio is normally two words, *ex officio*, without a hyphen; (c) *extramural* is correct; (d) extra-ordinary is also normally a single word, *extraordinary*.

9 (a) *far-flung* is correct; (b) inbuilt is normally *in-built*; (c) *in-group* is correct; (d) neoclassical is hyphenated to become *neo-classical*.

10 (a) noncommittal should be *non-committal*; (b) *non-deliver* is correct; (c) nonresistance should have a hyphen, *non-resistance*; (d) *non-smoker* is correct.

11 (a) *nonconformist* is correct; (b) nonsuch takes an 'e' to become *nonesuch*; (c) offkey takes a hyphen to become *off-key*; (d) *offshore* is correct.

12 (a) offpeak is usually hyphenated, *off-peak*; (b) on-looker is normally a single word, *onlooker*; (c) *onslaught* and (d) *on-stage* are both correct.

13 (a) *over-age* is correct; (b) over-shadow should be *overshadow*; (c) prearrange is usually hyphenated as *pre-arrange*; (d) *pre-natal* is correct.

14 (a) pre-occupy is normally a single word, *preoccupy*; (b) pro-noun is a single word, *pronoun*; (c) *re-enact* is correct; (d) *re-sign* is the correct spelling if the meaning is to sign again, but the spelling is *resign* if it means giving one's resignation.

15 (a) *self-respect* (b) *semi-detached* are both correct; (c) sub-committee should be a single word, *subcommittee*; (d) Anti-American should be *anti-American* — the prefix does not normally take a capital unless it is part of a proper name, as in Anti-Apartheid Movement.

15.2 *(page 191)*

1 This use of *take away* as a verb, not a noun, does not require a hyphen; *carry-all* (noun) is correct with a hyphen; sit-down, used here as a verb, should be *sit down* without a hyphen; *give-away* is correct as an adjective and broken down should similarly have a hyphen as *broken-down*.

2 The noun shut down should have a hyphen, as *shut-down*; *cut-back* (noun) and *sit-down* (adjective) are both correctly hyphenated; stand-by and fall-back should be separate words, *stand by* and *fall back*, since each is used here as a verb followed by a qualifying adverb.

3 Correct are *phone-in* and *goings-on*; play-back should be two words without a hyphen, *play back*, where it is used as here as a verb, not a noun; teach in should be *teach-in* where it is used here as a noun; far-off does not need a hyphen here and should be *far off*.

4 Correct use is made of *powerless*, *well-off* and *hangers-on*; home-less should be one word, *homeless*; in this instance, slow-down is used as a verb, not a noun, and so should be *slow down* without a hyphen.

5 Kickoff should be two hyphenated words, *kick-off*; *stand-off* is correct; both set-up and head-off are verbs here and should be without hyphens as *set up* and *head off*; knock out (adjective) should have a hyphen, as *knock-out*, though sometimes it is spelt *knockout*.

6 *Share-out* is correct but hand out should also have a hyphen, as *hand-out*, or, possibly, be the single word *handout*; *changeover* is correct (but *change-over* would be, too); also correct is *tip-offs*.

7 Correctly used are *plug-in*, *fold-up* and *checkout* (though *check-out* would also be correct); both clip on and foul up need hyphens in this context to become *clip-on* and *foul-up*.

8 *Fry-up* is correct; slapup should be *slap-up*; *diner-out* is correct; speed-up is used as a verb here and should be *speed up* without a hyphen; but washing up (noun) should be *washing-up*.

15.3 *(page 195)*

1   *Swing-wing* (adjective) is correct; turbo prop normally takes a
    hyphen to become *turbo-prop*; *stick-in-the-mud* is correct; take-off is
    used here as a verb, not a noun, so should be *take off* without a
    hyphen; *joy-riding* is correct; flarepath should be *flare-path*.

2   Grant aided should have a hyphen, *grant-aided*; *cheese-paring*
    (derived from cheese-pare) is correct, and so is *short-sighted*; this
    fall-out is a verb, not a noun, and so should be *fall out* without a
    hyphen; *corner-stones* is correct.

3   Break-out is used as a verb, not a noun, so should be *break out*
    without a hyphen; open-air with a hyphen is normally an adjective
    but it is used here as a separate adjective ('open') and noun ('air')
    and so should be *open air* without a hyphen; boxed-in has a hyphen
    when an adjective but here, as an adverb, it is normally *boxed in*;
    dust-up is correct.

4   *Hang-glide* is correct; common- sense with a hyphen is normally a
    compound adjective but when as here it forms a separate adjective
    and noun the correct spelling is *common sense* without a hyphen;
    crash-dive and *crash-landing* (derived from crash-land) are correct.

5   *Gold-plate* and *armour-plate* are correct; fashionplate should be two
    hyphenated words, *fashion-plate*; short sighted should be
    short-sighted; *lady-in-waiting* is correct.

6   *Souped-up* is correct; man of war should be *man-of-war*; fieldday
    should be hyphenated as *field-day*; *sea-to-air* is correct;
    highly-concentrated is not wrong in having a hyphen but the sense is
    clear without it so *highly concentrated* is sufficient and clearer;
    counter-attack is correct.

7   Check-up should be *check up* without a hyphen since it is a verb
    here, not a noun; *goings-on*, *theatre-goers* and *sang-froid* are
    correct; hankypanky should be *hanky-panky*; and volte face should
    be *volte-face*.

Chapter 17 *(page 213)*

1   analyses should be *analysis* (singular); *heir* is correct; weather should be *whether*; adviced should be *advised* (verb spelling, not noun).

2   coarse should be *course*; *site* is correct; bear should be *bare*; root should be *route*.

3   troupes (soldiers, not actors or circus performers) should be *troops*; *forth* is correct; board should be *bored*; wood should be *would*; pail should be *pale* (not the bucket).

4   knight should be *night*; pouring should be *poring* (studying, not spilling); *inquiry* and *check* are both correct; personnel should be *personal*.

5   *peace* is correct; peel should be *peal*, seamed should be *seemed*, and wining should be *whining*.

6   affect should be *effect* (for one thing, it's a noun); *exceeded* and *would* are correct; unaltared should be *unaltered*, and bean should be *been*.

7   bored (of directors) should be *board* (though you never know!); feint should be *faint*; *complimentary*, *team* and *crisis* are all correct.

8   *dependent* is correct; breaks should be *brakes*; tires is correct for Americans but in the UK the spelling should be *tyres*; insure should be *ensure* (again, though, not in the USA); *course* is correct.

9   unchequed should be *unchecked*; hoarse should be *horse*; heard should be *herd*; past should be *passed*; threw should be *through*; to should be *too*; vein should be *vain*; bridal should be *bridle*.

10 (in) *vain* is correct; too should be *two* (the number); would should be *wood*; *loose* is correct.

11 *brakes* is correct; jambed should be *jammed* (nothing to do with doorposts); bogey should be *bogie* (nothing to do with golf or ghosts); *said* is correct; notted needs a 'k' to become *knotted*.

12 seaming should be *seeming*; *teem* is correct, followed correctly by *team*; hire should be *higher*, wood should be *would*, and forth should be *fourth*.

13 bred should be *bread*, flower should be *flour*, and jamb should be *jam*; *cheap* is correct; holesome should be *wholesome*.

14 isle should be *aisle*, as in church, as *nave* correctly is; bough should be *bows*.

15 counsel should be *council*, and censor should be *censure*; *hordes* is correct; gorilla should be *guerilla* (or *guerrilla*), and rodes should be *roads*.